"Parenting is often the crucible in which we learn what we can and cannot control. Laura and Emily remind us that while we cannot control people or circumstances, we can control our perspective. They offer us a framework for motherhood that transcends time and culture but that also faithfully addresses us in the here and now. I'm thankful for this hope-filled book."

—**Jen Wilkin, director of classes and curriculum, The Village Church, and author of** *Women of the Word, None like Him,* **and** *In His Image*

"Emily and Laura are the best friends I wish I'd had during the difficult days of early motherhood, when my patience wore thin, my boredom loomed large, and my sense of worth and purpose became muddled. The wisdom they have to offer in the pages of this book is seasoned and scriptural."

—**Nancy Guthrie, author, Bible teacher, and ongoing pursuer of risen motherhood**

"*Risen Motherhood* delivers practical and present wisdom, anchored to timeless biblical truth. In *Risen Motherhood*, moms find empathy, encouragement, and the reminder that true hope for moms is through the transforming work of the gospel, alone."

—**Ruth Chou Simons, bestselling author of** *GraceLaced* **and** *Beholding and Becoming: The Art of Everyday Worship*

"This wonderful book offers deep sympathy and understanding to those who face the stress and challenges of motherhood. It also provides moms with a clear vision of their profound purpose and the hope they need to live vibrantly and meaningfully within this divine role. I highly recommend this book."

—**Sally Clarkson, bestselling author and host of the** *At Home with Sally* **podcast**

"If you are looking for practical tips on mothering and how-tos, this is not the book for you. But if you need to be refreshed and reminded that what Jesus accomplished on the cross and the grace available to us is sufficient for our daily mothering needs, you've come to the right place. *Risen Motherhood* will inspire you toward Bible reading, rest in the Savior, and joy—shored up by gospel truth—for the little years."

—**Trillia Newbell, author of** *Sacred Endurance, If God Is For Us,* **and** *God's Very Good Idea*

"Reading *Risen Motherhood* is like enjoying a long conversation with two girlfriends who will make you laugh out loud, comfort your tears, and faithfully speak life-giving words of truth to your soul. With wisdom and insight, Emily Jenson and Laura Wifler help moms connect the story line of Scripture to the daily realities of motherhood. This book is one every mom should read—I can't wait to share it with others!"

—**Melissa Kruger, director of women's content for The Gospel Coalition and the author of** *Walking with God in the Season of Motherhood*

"With *Risen Motherhood*, Emily and Laura offer us practical and theological insights on the nature of a mother's work and soul. This gem of a book explores how God is using sippy cups and play dates for His greater purposes. So come, read, and learn—not just how to rock the cradle but how to trust the One who rules the world."

—**Hannah Anderson, author of** *Humble Roots: How Humility Grounds and Nourishes Your Soul*

"Admittedly, I am not exactly the core audience for Risen Motherhood—the ministry or the book. That said, I always keep my ear to the ground for ministries I can grow to trust and then recommend to others. I'm delighted to say that for as long as I've followed Emily's and Laura's work I have benefitted from it. Even better, I have seen many Christian moms I know and love read their website, listen to their podcast, and grow through it. I'm thankful they've now added this book to the many channels through which they serve God by serving his people."

—**Tim Challies, bestselling author and popular blogger and book reviewer**

"It's easy to find friends who are quick to offer their opinion and advice. But it's rare to have friends who will point you back to the truth of the gospel of Jesus. Reading *Risen Motherhood* is like sitting down with those rare friends who offer truth—with grace and love—as you navigate the exhausting journey of parenting in this opinion-ridden culture."

—**Jerrad Lopes, founder of DadTired.com and author of** *Dad Tired…and Loving It*

"How does a Christian mom carry out her labors in raising children? By grace through faith in her crucified and risen Savior. The goal of Risen Motherhood ministry is to boldly announce and clearly explain the gospel of Jesus Christ—there's no better news for moms than this. I'm praying this book will strengthen weary hearts and fuel joyful worship of our risen Lord as moms flip through its pages."

—**Gloria Furman, author of** *Missional Motherhood* **and** *Treasuring Christ When Your Hands Are Full*

"This book is a breath of eternally fresh air. It's not another how-to-mother manual, but a beautiful explanation of very, very good news for every mom."

—**Quina Aragon, spoken word artist and author of** *Love Made: A Story of God's Overflowing, Creative Heart*

RISEN
MOTHERHOOD

EMILY JENSEN &
LAURA WIFLER

HARVEST HOUSE PUBLISHERS
EUGENE, OREGON

Cover design by Connie Gabbert Design + Illustration

Illustrations by Emilie Mann

Art Direction by Nicole Dougherty

Interior design by Rockwell Davis

Risen Motherhood

Copyright © 2019 by Emily Jensen and Laura Wifler
Published by Harvest House Publishers
Eugene, Oregon 97408
www.harvesthousepublishers.com

ISBN 978-0-7369-7622-0 (hardcover)
ISBN 978-0-7369-7623-7 (eBook)

Library of Congress Cataloging-in-Publication Data

Names: Jensen, Emily Warburton, author.
Title: Risen motherhood / Emily Jensen and Laura Wifler.
Description: Eugene : Harvest House Publishers, 2019.
Identifiers: LCCN 2019010802 (print) | LCCN 2019011444 (ebook) | ISBN 9780736976237 (ebook) | ISBN 9780736976220 (hardcover)
Subjects: LCSH: Mothers--Religious life. | Motherhood--Religious aspects--Christianity.
Classification: LCC BV4529.18 (ebook) | LCC BV4529.18 .J46 2019 (print) | DDC 248.8/431--dc23
LC record available at https://lccn.loc.gov/2019010802

Printed in the United States of America

19 20 21 22 23 24 25 26 27 / VP-RD / 10 9 8 7 6 5 4 3 2 1

For the Risen Motherhood community.
We're grateful to grow in the gospel alongside you.

ACKNOWLEDGMENTS

While our names are on the front of this book, the full weight of authorship is a heavy load we couldn't have carried without a small army of support.

To our husbands, Brad and Mike: You are the silent, sacrificial two who really made this book happen. We'll never forget your wholehearted support, enthusiasm, and encouragement to take time away to write. This book wouldn't exist without you both.

To our children, Lewis, Gabriel, Cal, Jones, and Eveline; Eli, Colette, and Eden: For better or worse, you've had a front-row seat to our sanctification and every lesson we share in the following pages. You are precious and dear to us—we love you more than you'll ever know.

To our parents and in-laws, Henry and Gayla, Dean and Dianne, Scott and Vicki: You've been some of our biggest cheerleaders. When we said we were writing a book, you had complete faith that we could do it, even when we were convinced otherwise. You asked what we needed, encouraged us to keep going, and provided hours of childcare!

To Grand Avenue Baptist Church and Naperville Presbyterian Church: You are our spiritual families, and we love you so much. Our ability to write something like this is, in part, a result of your shepherding as you poured the gospel into our hearts over the years.

To our team at the Risen Motherhood ministry: You gave us cheer emojis and hilarious GIFs the whole way and had no doubt this would be a thing. You've championed this like the best sisters could.

To those who read early copies of this and provided feedback: Karen Hodge, Abigail Dodds, Eric Schumacher, Jonathan Philgreen, and many more—you are kind and wise.

Our deep thanks to our agent, Andrew Wolgemuth, who skillfully led us through this process and advocated for us on every level. To our editor Kyle Hatfield and Harvest House, we're thankful to be your partners in the spread of the gospel. And to so many others who helped, encouraged, and cheered us on that we don't have the space to mention here, know that we are forever grateful. We noticed. It mattered.

Finally, the Lord. He planted the love of the gospel in our hearts long ago. He provided all the resources, space, mental energy, and more to do this, even when we felt completely depleted and insufficient for the task at hand.

We adore you, God. We hope this serves you.

Motherhood is hard.
One second, we think we're doing a good enough job;
the next, we feel like the worst mom on the planet.
Which is why we need the refreshing truth of the gospel
to be repeated over and over again,
giving us hope in the everyday moments.

We'd love to hear what you're learning as you read.
Share your thoughts with the hashtag
#risenmotherhoodbook.

CONTENTS

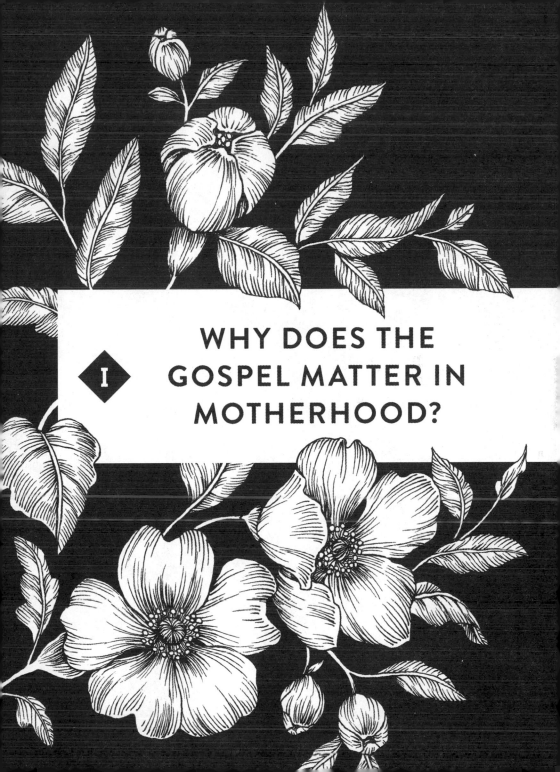

WHY DOES THE GOSPEL MATTER IN MOTHERHOOD?

I

RISEN MOTHERHOOD

Emily and Laura

Risen Motherhood started with potty training. It sounds silly, but as we both taught our oldest sons to use the potty, feeling weary of frequent clothing changes and the slow climb to success, we needed some tangible hope.

Since we lived five hours apart at the time, we discussed our experiences over a walkie-talkie app on our phones, leaving each other voice messages to respond to. We lamented the soiled laundry, celebrated the tiny victories, and shared our deeper struggles.

"It's just not clicking. I feel angry—is that normal?" one of us asked.

"Do you feel impatient? How do I give grace when it feels like he isn't making it to the potty *on purpose*?" the other asked.

We both wondered aloud, "Does the Bible address this? If Christ really changes everything, how does he change potty training? What does the gospel have to say about this?"

At first the answers were unclear. We started by swapping practical tips, finding humor in our battle stories. We fumbled, but we also dug deeper until we discovered the treasure of the gospel. We discussed our sin issues, building on each other's thoughts as the transforming work of Christ came clearly into focus. Only when we found our identity in Christ instead of the success of our children were we able to model his love to those who just couldn't get it. (It didn't always sound this clear and concise of course, but the gist of it was there.)

Through that process, our motherhood changed in a concrete way. Our children weren't suddenly dry all day, and we still swapped strategies, but the gospel proved more hopeful than any online article, more helpful than any book we could buy, and more sustaining than any quick fix we shared with one another.

It was a relief to find that it really is true—the gospel changes everything.

A Fix That Fails Us

We became first-time moms within nine months of each other, and although we didn't realize it at the time, we both entered motherhood with high expectations. We had visions of tidy living rooms, gourmet homemade dinners, peaceful walks with the stroller, and obedient children who loved Jesus (and their mamas).

We had a lot to learn, but we felt ready for the challenge. As we put together our baby registries—full of cute swaddles, high chairs, stylish (yet practical) diaper bags, and all the necessities—we were starry-eyed and optimistic. We knew there would be hard things, but we felt as prepared as we could be. After all, we were equipped with well-rounded registries, how-to books on motherhood, mom-friends who had gone before us, and the endless answers a Google search could provide.

Today, with eight kids between us, our optimistic expectations have toppled under the pressures of everyday life. Just like when we realized our carefully selected muslin swaddles were insufficient at holding our Houdini babies' arms in place, motherhood left us feeling inadequate, frustrated, and desperate for new solutions. We hastily searched for answers to where, when, and why our mothering went wrong. Although we found some helpful tips and practical strategies, in the end, the how-to books offered insufficient instructions, our mom-friends did things we didn't understand and didn't want to emulate, and Google (in all its millions of search results) didn't always hold the correct answers to our questions.

Other moms around us experienced a hole in their hopes for motherhood too. And it wasn't just our own mom-friends—it's a nearly universal experience in modern motherhood. According to a Barna Group study, 95 percent of moms say they need to do better in at least one area of life, 80 percent say they feel overwhelmed by stress, 70 percent say they don't get enough rest, and more than 50 percent feel overcommitted and dissatisfied by their balance of work and home life.[1]

If motherhood is supposed to be so wonderful—one of life's biggest blessings—why do we feel stressed, tired, dissatisfied, and overcommitted? If social media personalities, motherhood gurus, and book-writing experts hold the answers, why do we need more and more help?

Sometimes our response to "not enough" feelings in motherhood is to brush off our guilt instead of looking beneath it. Influencers, authors, and even our own friends and family tell us that simply because we are our children's loving moms, we *are* enough. Our well-intentioned efforts (however large or small) are all that's needed. We should stop worrying about the nagging guilt and create the life we want.

But deep down we still have this lurking feeling that we're missing the mark, and we don't know how to cope with it. So we joke and eye roll about our child's behavior. We post our mom-fails to social media. We let the mess be messy without bothering to clean it up. We tease the moms who seem more balanced or accomplished. When in doubt, we carve out more "me time" or escape into exercise, food, work, or social media. We lower the bar until our guilt is quieted.

If you are like us, these tactics fail to fully alleviate the guilt, stress, and pressures of everyday motherhood. Instead they send us on a confusing trial-and-error journey, where we never find rest. We can handle the striving for a while, but eventually something as simple as another potty training accident sends us over the edge. We're left dizzy, discouraged, and disarmed.

The mom culture at large and your natural desires want you to believe joy and success are won in the battle between the spilled milk and the kitchen floors, the stickers and the progress chart, your work and life balance, or your attitude and your child's behavior. But that's not it at all. This is a battle that's much

---

[1] The Barna Group, "Tired & Stressed, but Satisfied: Moms Juggle Kids, Career & Identity," *Barna*, September 1, 2018, https://www.barna.com/research/tired-stressed-but-satisfied-moms-juggle-kids-career-identity/.

bigger. A cosmic battle. It's a battle between the spirit and the flesh. Between good and evil. Between life and death.

It's a battle for your very soul.

Why We Need a Risen Motherhood

The world would have you believe the problem is that you can't *seem* to get your act together, but the reality is that you *can't* get your act together. Not in the sense that your sink always seems to be piled high with dishes, or you're not getting to the gym as often as you should, or you shoot random discipline strategies from the hip every 30 minutes. No, you can't get your act together because you're a sinner in need of a Savior.

Instead of showing our children the grace we've been shown, we build walls of rules and regulations to earn God's favor. Instead of serving our husbands out of love, we grumble in our hearts and keep a record of all the ways they've let us down in the past. Instead of spending time with our neighbors, we close up because we don't want the inconvenience or discomfort of getting to know someone new. Instead of reorienting our standards to God's, we look to our friends' or our news feeds. Instead of putting our hope in Christ, we put hope in our own efforts and comfort—living for naptime, bedtime, when Daddy gets home, when we get to leave for work, or when we'll have time to zone out on our phones.

In the short term, we are far too easily motivated by the promise of a Netflix binge, the sweet treat in the pantry, or the upcoming girls' trip. But none of these things last beyond a moment, and they don't cure the problem deep within us. We cannot will ourselves into finding joy in motherhood because we cannot will ourselves into the obedience or love God requires of us. If we're to find true, lasting joy in our motherhood journey, what we need is the work of Jesus Christ.

We don't need the world's version of motherhood; we need a risen motherhood, transformed by the resurrection of our Lord and Savior. We need his shed blood if we're going to shed our guilt and failures. We need his fullness to fill us where we are empty. We need his sacrifice and hurt so we can sacrifice for others

WE NEED A RISEN
MOTHERHOOD

until it hurts. We need his wounds to cure our wounds. We need his atonement to atone once and for all for our sins. We need his death to give us life.

Understanding Risen Motherhood

These things sound nice. You may be nodding along while still wondering, "What exactly does that mean? We need his wounds to cure our wounds? How is that going to help me *right now*?"

That's exactly the question we hope to answer in this book. We're not giving parenting advice. We're not looking back with wisdom from the experience of years. We're moms looking at these problems with you, drawing a big line from the church sermon to the snotty nose that needs to be wiped (again).

In the remainder of part 1 (chapters 2 and 3), we'll talk through the gospel story and look at its application to the general concept of motherhood. We'll examine how this redemptive narrative gives us hope beyond the temporary fixes the world provides as we orient our lives around God's Word.

In part 2 we'll tackle 14 common topics moms face, exploring a specific application of the gospel for each subject, following the pattern of creation, fall, redemption, and consummation. For believers especially, this is not empty repetition. It's a story arc with the power to revive our faith, pointing our eyes back to Christ. This pattern will be a familiar friend to you if you've followed the Risen Motherhood ministry.

God's overall design for motherhood is unchanging and universal, but each mom's life is unique because of her culture, background, life experience, socioeconomic status, and more. There are endless ways to look at each topic in this book and apply the gospel. We've chosen just one way for each chapter. To cover everything about each topic would require an entire library!

In part 3 we'll encourage you to grow in your love for God by developing Bible literacy and gospel fluency, even during your child's little years. We'll send you off equipped with methods for applying the gospel to whatever you're facing in your everyday life.

Risen Motherhood Is for You

We're just two moms with two life experiences. We are still learning and growing. Our kids sometimes wake up too early and stay up too late. They throw tantrums in public places. They wear four layers of costumes at once and would like to have a continual stream of candy handed to them throughout the day. We have common struggles, but we also have a common desire to press beyond commiseration into Christlikeness. We're shocked at how much we've learned in our short years of motherhood, and we're confident we'll learn even more after we publish this book!

Through this book we hope you'll be encouraged and that you'll gain a greater ability to see God and your own life through gospel lenses. We pray this book will springboard discussions with others in your church or community so you can think deeply about topics you may not have considered before. If the two of us can learn to see life through a gospel lens between breakfast and bath time, so can you. But it takes practice. And it requires intentionality, diligence, growth, and admitting you need to make course corrections. But we'll also attest that God is faithful, and he will help a mother who longs to live out the gospel in her everyday life.

This book is for any mother who has ever wondered if God cares about the fact that she's cleaning out the cheese crackers ground into the carpet. For the mother who feels as though she has reached her limit but doesn't know where to turn for help. For the mother who secretly fears her world will crumble if she doesn't keep all the plates spinning. For the mother who is lonely and can't hear the call to life in God's community. For the mother who is grieving through the deepest kind of heartache and is crying out, "God, do you see this? Do you hear me?"

This book is for every mom who is asking, "Does the gospel matter to motherhood?"

Oh, friend, the gospel changes everything.

Let's get started.

WHAT IS THE GOSPEL?

Emily and Laura

Many of us feel a disconnect between our Sunday-morning faith and our Monday-morning mom life. We wonder how hymns, prayers, and Bible reading intersect school lunches, footie pajamas, and full-blown, on-the-ground, tear-filled tantrums. We have our Christian faith, and then we have real life. The church and the Bible feel outdated—good for Sundays and nostalgia, but that's about it.

But these two aspects of life are part of a bigger story, a cosmic battle, even when we can't see it. It's a bit like being downstairs quietly washing dishes, listening to music and humming along, while upstairs the kids are in a Nerf gun battle, shooting things off shelves, jumping on beds, and practicing their parkour moves. We feel like time is quietly passing, but in reality, an epic war is raging right over our heads. Only the sounds of furniture bouncing and ceiling joists shaking cause us to look up with wonder.

We admit, amid diaper changes, babysitting swaps, and bill paying, this cosmic reality is hard to fathom. That's why it's so easy to put faith and life in separate boxes. But really, our faith and life should be woven together, inseparable. Like Play-Doh in the carpet threads, it's impossible to tell where one ends and the other begins. But to do that, we must understand the story we're in and the role we play. We must know it from the beginning to the end.

This story is commonly known as the gospel. The gospel is the good news that God sent his Son, Jesus, to save sinners by his sacrifice, making a way for them to have eternal life with God. That's the shorthand version, but there's so much more to know and understand.

Depending on your background, you might view the gospel message in different ways. Perhaps you have heard this story so many times it makes your eyes glaze over. Or possibly you see it as a one-time message for sinners—an entry ticket to heaven. Maybe you're resistant to the message, thinking it brainwashes people into ultraconservative religious thinking that dampens the joy of real life. Or maybe you shrink back, thinking that before receiving such good news, you need to put on your best clothes and rid your life of anything undesirable. Or perhaps you are new to the faith, and the gospel feels so fresh and exciting, you can't seem to get enough of it. Or maybe you're like us—the gospel story has been a faithful friend by your side for many years as you've grown in your love for it.

The gospel might seem like different things to different people, but the truth is always the same. It's a beautiful tale of love, redemption, joy, and hope. It's the biggest theme in Scripture—simple enough for the ears of a toddler and deep enough for a lifetime of scholarly research.[1] Understanding the gospel in its basic parts is key to the Christian life, both for salvation (deliverance from sin's penalty in exchange for eternal life with God) and for sanctification (a fancy word for becoming more like Jesus in our heart and actions even though we're already delivered from sin's penalty). It's key to getting your faith and daily life out of two separate boxes and intertwining them into one big expression of worship. This story is more than relevant to your everyday life. In fact, your life *depends* on it.

You have probably heard this story before, but please resist the temptation to skip ahead. We all need the refreshing truth of the gospel to be repeated over

---

[1] Adapted from Saint Augustine's famous quote, "The Bible is shallow enough for a child not to drown, yet deep enough for an elephant to swim."

and over again. It's the foundation for everything else we're going to explore in this book and everything God will do in our lives through Christ.

The Gospel Story

CREATION

Before the stars, the sun, the moon, and the earth were created, God was present. He is three persons in one: the Father, the Son, and the Holy Spirit. As an overflow of this good and loving union, God created the heavens, the earth, and everything in it. He made the first people (Adam and Eve) in his image and placed them in the beautiful Garden of Eden, where he walked with them and enjoyed a loving relationship with them. The triune God called everything he made "very good."[2]

Adam and Eve were created male and female, with a united purpose on Earth as they enjoyed, loved, and worshipped God: to be fruitful and multiply and to reign on the earth.[3] It sounds easy, right?

FALL

Before any of our children took a toy from their sibling and shoved them to the ground, there was the first sin. God had an opponent—like an evil villain in the bedtime stories we read to our children—but this villain isn't pretend. He's a fallen angel named Satan, whose mission is to usurp God and steal his glory. The cosmic battle begins.

Although God gave Adam and Eve everything good in the garden to eat, one tree was off-limits—the tree of the knowledge of good and evil. They couldn't eat from the tree because if they did, they would die. But thanks to Satan, who entered the scene as a tricky serpent, they started to question God's instruction.

Satan, a master of exchanging God's truth for lies, tempted Adam and Eve

---

[2] Genesis 1:31.

[3] Genesis 1:28.

THE GOSPEL
MEETS US IN
EVERYDAY LIFE

with the forbidden tree.[4] Filled with selfish desire and consumed by the idea that this one thing might make them more fulfilled, Adam and Eve ate the fruit. Their disobedience had devastating consequences for all of creation, ushering in death, pain, destruction, and suffering.

Humanity had a serious problem. They were cut off from God. Now banished from the garden with a severed relationship to God, Adam and Eve were sent eastward with a curse hanging over the heads, a noose of death over them and all creation. Their sin infected every human who came after them—including us.

REDEMPTION

But God didn't banish them without promising their rescue. Adam and Eve deserved to drop dead on the spot, but God offered the gracious, undeserved hope of a Promised One who would someday crush the serpent. Thousands of years later, Jesus, God's Son, came as a baby who grew into a man, living a perfect life so he could be the perfect sacrifice. He was unjustly accused and tried, resulting in a death sentence that he humbly accepted. On the cross, Christ willingly endured undeserved torture, shame, and death in place of sinners. But his death was not the end of the story.

On the third day, the firstfruits of redemptive life followed death's defeat. Jesus did what no one thought possible—he arose a conquering hero from the grave! He provided freedom from the curse of sin that invades our hearts, and he gave those who believe in him eternal and abundant life. We still die a physical death, but believers will live spiritually in the presence of God until Jesus returns to resurrect their physical bodies and create a new world. Until then, he has sealed his people with the Holy Spirit, who comes to live in all who confess belief in this story of redemption, helping them persevere until Christ's return.

CONSUMMATION

One day Jesus will return, resurrecting the dead in Christ, bringing the living

---

[4] Genesis 3:1-4.

believers to himself, and transforming them to be like himself. God will make the whole earth new and oversee the final judgment. Eden had the potential for perfection, but the new earth will *be* perfect. Satan, the enemy, will be defeated once and for all. He'll be thrown into the lake of fire, never again able to tempt us with his lies and tainted promises. Those who believed in the world's answers, hoped in themselves, and refused to bow to Christ as Lord will be condemned eternally. On that day, followers of Christ will reign with him and dwell with God. We'll no longer struggle with distracted hearts, lukewarm affection, and misplaced worship. On the day of the final defeat of darkness, we'll fully dwell with the King of lights forever with eternal joy, peace, and companionship—more alive than we've ever been.

Already but Not Yet

Many years have passed since the first sin, but moms still endure life under the curse. We're used to battles of every kind—battles with sweaty kids who don't want to get back into the car, battles with other moms over the right snacks to feed our children, battles with our never-ending laundry pile, battles with the bills that come month after month. And we battle deeper, harder things too—the empty womb, the anger in our hearts that feels impossible to control, the sour marriage, the selfish spirit, the empty bank account, and the wayward child. We feel stuck in a world much like Narnia under the White Witch's rule—"Always winter but never Christmas."[5]

Just like the mom washing the dishes in peace and quiet, not realizing the Nerf gun battle raging on the second floor, we see the light fixture shake and sense that something is wrong. The echoes of concern stir our souls, causing us to second-guess our reality. But Satan makes every effort to distract us, conceal the real battle, and lead us off course. We're duped into thinking we can figure out how to save ourselves...or maybe just survive by making ourselves a little

---

[5] C.S. Lewis, *The Chronicles of Narnia: The Lion, the Witch and the Wardrobe* (New York, NY: Harper Collins, 1950), 118.

more comfortable for a time. So we tweak our routines, fix our outward behavior, or find a crutch to lean on, but nothing lasts.

This is where the gospel meets everyday life.

Right now, we're living between redemption and consummation. This is what people mean by "living in the already but not yet." Christ has already defeated the enemy Satan, but we have not yet seen the entire plan of redemption come to fruition. Sin remains in our hearts and the world around us, but there is also new life, growth, change, and good fruit. If we turn our eyes to Christ and believe the gospel, we don't have to keep striving or trying to numb the pain from the penalty of sin. We can rest because Christ is our Champion seated beside God.

If you trust in Christ, the power that raised him from the dead is the same power in your daily life. The Holy Spirit provides what you need to be patient, kind, loving, long-suffering, faithful, and gentle toward your husband, children, and others around you. He allows you to see that motherhood isn't just made up of long days and tedious work—motherhood is made up of a million tiny moments for worship. All of life is about growing in Christlikeness, sharing God's love, and seeing Christ's kingdom established here on Earth.

It's a slow, humble, and difficult process, but we're meant to live out this purpose in the everyday moments. Even when motherhood feels empty and void, when the work feels trite and blasé, we remember that we're part of a greater story. We just have to filter our world through the proper lens. We have to see the ceiling shaking from the Nerf gun combat, drop our dishrags, run up the stairs, and engage the real battle.

Applying the Gospel to Your Everyday Life

Now that we know (and hopefully believe) the gospel story, how do we apply it? Why does eternal life matter when your children refuse the meal you spent all day planning and preparing? Why does heaven matter when you're considering whether to work outside the home after having a baby? What's the point of the promise of new life when your basement floods and you must fight with the insurance company to get it covered?

We get it. Sometimes the concept of the story remains disconnected from the demands of this moment. These questions birthed the Risen Motherhood ministry—and this book.

For the remainder of the book, we'll apply the gospel story to many areas of motherhood. We'll do this by looking at four major parts of the gospel story, asking essential questions about each part. Here's a quick look at the overarching thought process and questions we asked ourselves as we wrote each chapter. These might be helpful as you learn to apply the gospel to your own unique situation, but we'll look at that more closely at the end of this book.

CREATION

The creation aspect of the gospel reminds us that God is the main character, and he designed everything to function a certain way for our good and his glory. All our satisfaction and purpose comes from him, and our lives are to be lived as worship to God.

When we consider an issue related to motherhood through the lens of creation, we'll ask questions like these: How did God originally intend for this to be? How would it function without sin and brokenness? How does it reflect the beauty of who he is?

FALL

This aspect of the gospel reminds us that we inherited a sin nature through Adam and that all of creation is broken. Life no longer functions according to God's good design but instead is painful and deviant. Because of God's common grace in creation, there are still good things to see and enjoy, but the fall has implications for our daily lives.

When we consider the fall's impact on an issue in motherhood, we'll ask questions like these: How has sin and brokenness in this situation or area

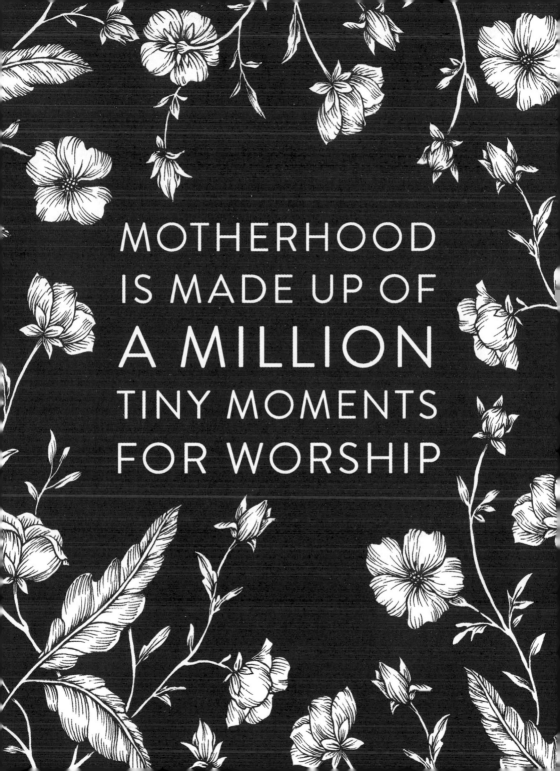

MOTHERHOOD
IS MADE UP OF
A MILLION
TINY MOMENTS
FOR WORSHIP

diverged from God's design? How is it keeping us all from living according to God's good plan? How has sin infiltrated my thoughts, words, or actions?

REDEMPTION

The redemptive aspect of the gospel reminds us that God made a way to reconcile the problem of sin and death, allowing a way back to himself, giving people life for their good and his glory. This was done through the perfect life and atoning sacrifice of his Son, Jesus, who defeated death as he rose from the dead and later ascended into heaven. He sent a Helper, the Holy Spirit, to seal his followers and help them until he returns. In the meantime, we've been given a mission—to love God, love others, and make disciples of all nations.

When we consider how redemption impacts an issue in motherhood, we'll ask questions like these: What do I need to repent of in this situation? How does my freedom from sin empower me to obey God and adhere to his original design? How can I steward this situation or relationship in a way that honors God and is a means of evangelism or discipleship?

CONSUMMATION

The consummation of God's kingdom reminds us to look ahead. We mourn now, but we have hope in a future without tears.[6] Jesus will return for final judgment, and at that time, God will make all things new. Believers will live on a new earth with God forever, where everything and everyone will worship him and live according to his design for eternity. Those who didn't trust in his Son as their payment for sin in this life will suffer eternal separation and punishment.

When we consider how consummation impacts an issue in motherhood, we'll ask questions like these: How does the assurance of future hope change my perspective and the way I have hope right now? What do I have to lose in this life? Where can I anchor my joy amid my ever-changing circumstances?

The gospel is infinitely beautiful and complex, so there are various ways to consider it, ask questions about it, and apply it to daily living. We hope as you

---

[6] 1 Thessalonians 4:13.

ask these questions alongside us in this book, you'll begin to see how it powerfully transforms all we do in motherhood and will find innumerable connections between your faith and daily life.

Let's start by understanding how the gospel transforms the overall concept of motherhood.

DISCUSSION QUESTIONS

1. How has your background contributed to your feelings about or understanding of the gospel?

2. Have you believed the good news and put your faith in Christ's death and resurrection? If so, what hope do you have today and forever?

3. Where have you been doing battle in motherhood? Considering what you've learned about the gospel, describe the actual battleground and the real enemy.

GOD'S PURPOSE FOR MOTHERHOOD

Emily and Laura

When we're about to give birth for the first time or adopt a child, we naturally gather information about motherhood. We reflect on our own mothers and grandmothers. We prod for stories about how our mothers-in-law did things when our husbands were little. We search the internet, asking our seasoned mom-friends for advice, attending mom meet-ups in our community, joining conversations in online mom forums, and observing social media. We listen to our own gut instincts and set our personal standards for what a good mom looks like. From all of this, we shape our own paradigms of motherhood and make our own conclusions for the role and purpose of a mom.

We can certainly learn some helpful things from others, but God's Word explains the definitive purpose of motherhood, and our understanding of his character and design should inform our understanding of what it means to be a mom.

God's Design for Motherhood

Man was created first, and then woman was created from him to be his helper.[1] She wasn't a helper in the sense of being less valuable than Adam; rather,

[1] Genesis 2:18-22.

he needed help—it wasn't good for him to be alone.[2] On his own, he was missing something in his ability to live out God's instructions. There would be no good work or future generations without woman. Eve would be a complementary image-bearer with equal value, but as a female, she imaged God in different ways than Adam did.

In the original language, Eve's name sounds like "life." The account in Genesis says, "The man called his wife's name Eve, because she was the mother of all living."[3] And right there, in the third chapter of the Bible, we find the concept of motherhood.

The word "mother" has multiple layers of meaning. Eve had the potential to be a biological mother, but she also represented a spiritual purpose all women can relate to: to invest in and nurture the family of God as life-givers.[4] In the context of the whole Bible, spiritual mothers play essential roles in the redemptive story. We see them passing on God's promises to future generations, boldly protecting the lineage of God's people, training and discipling those around them, heralding the good news, and more.

For the sake of this book, we're going to focus primarily on God's design and purpose for mothers in the biological or adoptive sense, as you're probably reading this book because you're curious about your responsibility and mission as a mom with children in your home. While the two have some overlapping purposes, we'll observe this design going forward.

God's physical design for Eve tells us something about his purpose for motherhood. Eve had a womb—a perfect environment for growing a child until he or she entered the world. After birth, Eve could feed the baby with a perfect cocktail of nutrients in her breast milk. A baby could be nurtured by her bosom, have skin-to-skin contact, and experience necessary physical love at least every few hours for the first years of life. Because filling the earth was a part of God's instructions for Adam and Eve, this pattern likely would have

---

[2] Genesis 2:18.   [3] Genesis 3:20.

[4] For further reading, see Susan Hunt, *Spiritual Mothering* (Wheaton, IL: Crossway, 1993); Gloria Furman, *Missional Motherhood* (Wheaton, IL: Crossway, 2016).

repeated itself many times. Bearing and raising children would have impacted her rhythms of work and how her days were ordered and filled.

There is a spiritual design to motherhood as well. Throughout the rest of Scripture, we see moms are essential to the spiritual upbringing and formation of their children's character. Together, moms and dads are tasked with teaching children the redemptive story along with God's character and law. Parents should train their children in wisdom (discerning right from wrong) and faithfully discipline with love and self-control. All of this is done with the hope of seeing their children walk in righteousness. Myriads of books are available about the ins and outs and practical how-tos for today, but overall, a mother is meant to model God's love, instruction, and discipline for her children.

This gets to the heart of motherhood: God's design, both physically and spiritually, reflects the heart of the greatest Life Giver to the world. He is the ultimate Creator of life, the ultimate nurturer and provider, and the compassionate, gentle one who supplies our needs when—like our own babies—our only capacity is to cry for help. God's love for his people is compared to the fierce, protective compassion a nursing mother has for her own helpless child.[5] This is how he cares for us! As a mother shows mercy to her helpless child, he shows mercy to helpless people. God also lovingly trains and disciplines us as his children, making us more into the likeness of Jesus.

What does this design for motherhood mean to us when we're struggling? First, it moves our heart's desire for satisfaction from "how we mother" to finding it in God, the true Life Giver and Helper. Second, it doesn't allow us to just lower the bar or brush past God's design. Instead it compels us to understand why we struggle and where we find hope. It bids us to keep walking through the narrative of the gospel to see God's good news for hurting moms.

Why Can't We Achieve God's Design?

Eve, the woman who was to be the mother of life, ushers in death when she

---

[5] Isaiah 49:15.

disobeys God in the garden. The curse touches everything. We live in sinful and broken circumstances due to things inside and outside our control.

Physically, the womb we hope to fill may not be able to hold a child. If it does, that child might be born with various health complications. Childbirth is a dangerous business for both mother and baby, filled with pain, blood, travail, and groaning, giving women reason to fear when bringing life into the world.[6] A mom won't always be married. A mom won't always be able to breast-feed. A mom won't always be able to keep her child. A mom may have necessary demands pull her away so she can't nurture or care for her child the way God has designed as they grow and mature.

The fall impacts motherhood in spiritual ways too. By her sin, Eve leaves a legacy of spiritual death, which is contrary to fulfilling the creation mandate God gave them to expand his kingdom on Earth. In every area, we exchange worship of the Creator for the worship of the created.[7] We even worship our ability to be good moms. Sin and its heartaches make women want to turn away from God in despair instead of turning to him in joy.

Children disobey parents. Generations engage in habitual sins. People envy, steal, murder, and pervert human relationships in every way. The hand of a mother and a father might bring abuse and hate instead of love, training, and nurture.

Our hearts are consistently troubled by underlying currents of guilt and shame. We fear we'll never measure up, so we measure ourselves by the lives of others, both online and in real life. Motherhood doesn't just mean smiles and sleepless nights, but also shooting glances into your mom-friend's baby bag and noticing she has glass bottles when you have plastic. Even the slightest differences make us insecure, defensive, and judgmental.

This is an ugly place for life.

Is There Any Hope?

As moms living with sinful hearts in a broken world, we struggle and toil,

---

[6] Genesis 3:16.

[7] Romans 1:25.

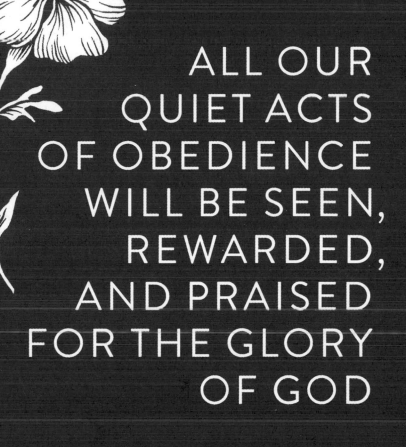

ALL OUR
QUIET ACTS
OF OBEDIENCE
WILL BE SEEN,
REWARDED,
AND PRAISED
FOR THE GLORY
OF GOD

but in Christ, we're not left without hope. God overcomes the curse by giving people another way to experience birth—not through a physical womb, but through the Holy Spirit.[8] While a mother gives birth through physical groaning, sweat and tears, her water breaking, and the shedding of her blood—Jesus makes a way for life through his physical torture, sweat and tears in the garden, water pouring from his side, and his pure, perfect blood shed for us on the cross. The story of the crucified Christ is the best birth story ever told, with elements that parallel the gospel picture in each labor and delivery room.

But Jesus doesn't deliver babies—he delivers captives.[9]

Through his death and resurrection, Christ has perfectly fulfilled everything expected of us as mothers. He's been the "true and better mom," so to speak, and he sends a Helper to make us more like him. If we are in Christ, God's design is something our new nature longs to live by because our Father is good, and obedience to him brings us joy.

Until Christ returns, mothers have the mission of duplicating life and being fruitful through the Great Commission by the power of the Holy Spirit.[10] Our mothering should point our husbands, children, churches, and communities toward knowing and loving the same gospel we love. We are to make the best use of the time we have, aligning our lives to God's design laid out in his Word.

A Final Birth Is Coming

The struggles we face today are not forever. If we are found in Christ, all our quiet acts of obedience will be seen, rewarded, and praised for the glory of God, and all our sins are paid for by the blood of Christ. Those who never trust in Jesus' sacrifice will have their debt come due, with the payment being eternal punishment. But there will be yet another birth story as God makes all things forever new, where we will live eternally with him and for him and through him.

The final birth reminds us this life is not all there is. Yes, what happens during

---

[8] John 3:3; 1 Peter 1:22-23.

[9] Luke 4:18.

[10] Matthew 22:36-40; 28:16-20.

these days and years on this earth matters, but all of it is building toward something much bigger than what we see here. Our days under the sun are refining, pruning, growing, and maturing us to become more like Christ, preparing for us a future weight of glory when God births his new and final creation with life abundant. This birth story is the only one that will set your soul free from the grip of fear, struggle, and failure as a mom. If you believe it—and understand it—it shifts your entire paradigm as a mother, delivering your captive heart into the arms of a loving Savior.

Risen Motherhood in the Daily Life of a Mom

With God's design for life and godliness in mind, we can consider various aspects of motherhood in light of the gospel, which is what we'll do in the next section. Using the pattern of creation, fall, redemption, and consummation that we walked through in the last chapter, we'll apply the gospel to everything from dishes to devotions to disabilities. Remember, every mom's personality, sin issues, and circumstances are unique, and there are endless ways to look at each topic and apply the gospel. For the purposes of this book, we've chosen just one common angle.

We hope this next section offers food for thought that sparks meditation on Scripture, a deeper love for God, a fuller hope in salvation, a greater motivation toward obedience, and a truer need for conversation in community with other believers. It's not exhaustive, but it is a start. Let's get going.

DISCUSSION QUESTIONS

1. Can you summarize God's purpose for motherhood in your own words? How does that compare with your idea of the ideal mom?

2. In what ways have you personally seen the effects of the fall in your motherhood? Where does God want you to turn during hard things, when you feel discouraged about your inability to measure up?

3. Where do you need God's help to live out his purpose today?

II

GOSPEL HOPE FOR THE EVERYDAY MOMENTS OF MOTHERHOOD

THE GOSPEL AND OUR
HEART ATTITUDES

Laura

I t was another late night of work for my husband. Outside the snow fell in a heavy blanket, which meant I had been home alone with my three kids all day to avoid the roads. We had done all the fun things I could possibly think of: playing with puzzles, books, and Play-Doh; painting with watercolors; building a fort under the dining room table; and playing pretend paleontologists in the living room. You name it, we'd done it. At five that evening, I waved the white flag and told the kids that because the baby was napping, we could put a movie on and have snack plates for dinner.

To be honest, I had been looking forward to this time all day. I felt I earned the break because I'd been so involved and invested in my children. I had been a good mom, a fun mom…dare I say a Pinterest mom! My husband was in a season of working 12-plus hour days, six or seven days a week. I mean, didn't I deserve a little credit for my sacrifice?

As I clicked on the TV, I asked the kids what they wanted to watch, and immediately the bickering broke out. She wanted dinosaurs, he wanted dragons, and neither one was giving in. As I tried to stop their fighting, my voice rose louder and louder, and suddenly I could feel my pent-up frustration release from a day cooped up at home. I made empty threats about not watching any show at all if they couldn't stop fighting. "TV is a privilege," I told them as I picked a completely different show and walked away.

In the other room, I crumbled. I knew even as the words came out of my mouth that I had been unjust and unkind to my children. I had taken out my misplaced frustration on them, but in the moment, I didn't care. I could easily pull out 15 reasons I earned quiet time while the kids watched their show, but as I ran them through my head, I realized they were all prideful and self-centered. I confessed it all to God, pleading for him to show up in the areas I was weak.

I stood up and walked back into the living room to apologize to my children. I paused the show (much to their vocal dismay). "I'm sorry," I told them. "Will you forgive me?" I told them I didn't want to be that kind of mother, and thankfully, because of Christ, I didn't have to be.

Culture's Message: Change Your Circumstances

I think we can all agree that motherhood is hard and life can bring out the worst in us. But culture would attest that if we have the right systems in place, we can always be the best version of ourselves. During an exercise program I recently worked out to, the trainer yelled, "Give me 30 minutes of your day, and I promise you'll be a better person, wife, husband, or parent!" We're told we're in the driver's seat. If we try a little harder, we'll finally gain control over our circumstances, and our worries, fears, and frustrations will melt away.

A mom's answer to her hurting heart and emotional outbursts is simple: "You just need to get up earlier. Buy a better planner. Rotate your toys more often. Make a chore chart. Implement a housecleaning system. Find a personal assistant for your growing home-business. Use a think-it-over corner. Eat less sugar. Count to 20 and chant a calming mantra before you speak."

And while there is value in staying organized, implementing wise systems, and making smart adjustments to your life, the subtle lie underneath taunts our hearts with false promises: Do this, and you'll have control! Do that, and you'll be a nicer mother!

So as moms, we wake up each day ready to do whatever it takes to put away the anger, stress, and worry—hoping to dig deep for patience and peace somewhere within. We believe if we can just get a little more control over our outside environment, we won't feel so temperamental on the inside. We hang inspirational quotes on our letter board, start a new weekly meal-prep plan we saw on Instagram, and attempt a new discipline strategy we heard on a recent podcast.

But as the day wears on, each thing fails us. Our patience thins, our peace wears out, and we go through the common cycle of frustration, despair, and guilt. No matter what we implement or how much we muscle our emotions, we're still a mess. Stressed out and out of control, we look for somewhere to throw the blame other than on ourselves. Doling out unfair punishments, justifying worry and anxiety, and living with regret for what we've just said, we're unhappy with ourselves but not quite sure what else to change.

Sometimes in motherhood, we crave control and comfort so much we worship them. We chase all the things that might give us command over our home, husbands, and children, thinking that if we just find the magic ticket, motherhood will be easier and we'll finally be peaceful, patient, and kind. We'll finally be the women we wish we were.

But no matter how much effort we put into it, we can't seem to tame the dragon nature inside that roars for control and success.

What we need is a dragon slayer.

The Gospel Message

CREATION: Created for Worship

Watch any child long enough, and you'll know that humans are made for worship. Like a toddler in the toy aisle throwing a tantrum because you won't buy them the purple kitty with the enormous eyes, their outward rage is only a sign of the war of worship in their hearts. God made us in his own image for his glory, which means we are created by God, for God, and for worship.[1] As

---

[1] Genesis 1:27; Isaiah 43:7.

humans, worship is something we do all day, every day. It cannot separate from the human experience; it's part of our very being.

Existing long before Adam and Eve or any other human, God is the only one worthy of our worship. He is the Creator; we are the created.[2] In the Genesis account, we see an intentional design to the earth, showing he is sovereign, he is in control, and he sustains all.

He is God and the only one worthy of worship.

FALL: The Dragon's Deceit

Created to worship, we crave it. In the fall, Satan (later described as a dragon[3]) deceived Eve when she had a craving to worship herself over God. She doubted God's promises, thinking if she could just get control of her circumstances, she might be better off. Very quickly her circumstances only got worse. Separated from her Creator, the perpetual wandering and roaming of the human heart for worship began.[4]

Now consciously and unconsciously, we look for functional idols to replace God's rightful position in our lives. This can take a thousand forms—like money, fame, obedient robot children, a magical pair of mom jeans that hide the post-partum pooch—but most often, that idol is simply a worship of self. We are now our own biggest problem, and most of the time, we live in denial of how rebellious our hearts truly are. We raise our voice when we feel unheard. We defend when we feel wronged. We worry when we lose control. The dragon whispers deceptions in our ears: "Try harder. Be better. Maintain control. Find the willpower within."

So like Adam and Eve pointing fingers when God asked what happened,[5] we protect ourselves at all costs, looking for any way to avoid pain, difficulty, or failure when life doesn't go the way we want. But because we no longer live

---

[2] Ephesians 3:9; Colossians 1:16.

[3] Revelation 12:7.

[4] Genesis 3:8.

[5] Genesis 3:9-13.

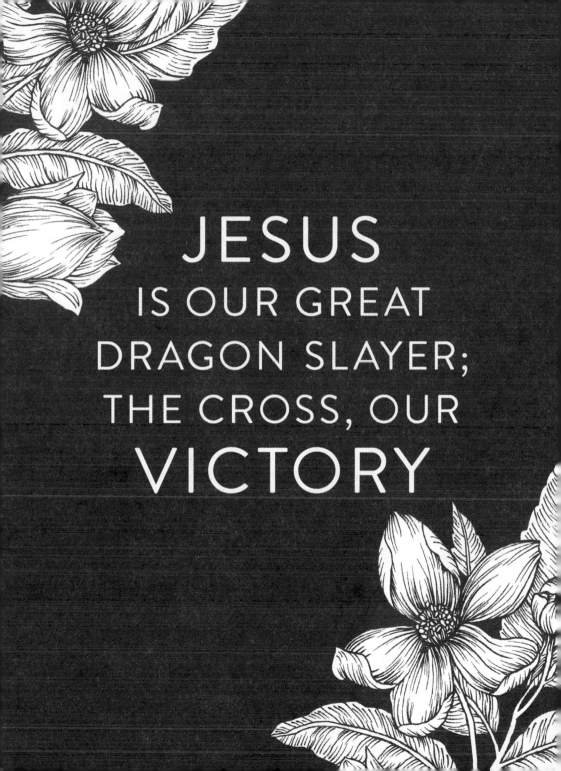

JESUS
IS OUR GREAT
DRAGON SLAYER;
THE CROSS, OUR
VICTORY

in communion with our true source of worship, all our worldly solutions fail us, and our misplaced worship reveals itself in the form of worry, anger, anxiety, impatience, and more.

By listening to the dragon, we have become like the dragon.

REDEMPTION: The Great Dragon Slayer

Of all the great heroes in the Bible, none could defeat Satan the dragon. Instead of resisting temptation, Eve worshipped her own plan for her future over God's design. Instead of trusting God, Moses fled to the desert valuing his own comforts and rejecting God's purpose for him. Instead of believing in God's sovereignty, David idolized his own desires for pleasure and protection—even to the point of taking another's life.

We can't defeat the dragon on our own either. The weak, wandering heart of a human could never win the cosmic battle. Thankfully, God sent a warrior King to rescue us from the dragon's lies. Through Christ's victory over death, he slew the dragon once and for all, shattering his deception and lies and arming us to stand against his schemes. Jesus did what we could never do—he lived a perfect life of worship to the Father in our stead, resisting every temptation and accusation.

Jesus is our great dragon slayer; the cross, our victory.

Because of this, the Holy Spirit is transforming us from the inside out. We no longer need to try to control our external circumstances or muster up a good attitude, a peaceful presence, or a kind word because what we need has already been given to us. Christ is our patience. Christ is our peace. Christ is our kindness. Christ is our joy. No matter our circumstances, we know God is in control, not us, and we can trust his promises when things don't go our way.

In Christ's power, we can tame the dragon nature inside.

CONSUMMATION: The Dragon's Final Defeat

Someday the dragon will be destroyed forever. He has temporary rule on the earth, but we know when Christ returns and we unite with him in heaven,

Satan will be defeated for good.[6] At that time we'll no longer struggle from worship whiplash. In eternity we will be caught up in the presence of our Savior to finally and fully enjoy his glory and goodness, and we will live in uninhibited worship of our God.[7]

Until then God uses the circumstances in our lives to soften and shape our hearts to reflect himself. When we find our joy in him and his promises, we can image Christ as we respond with graciousness and kindness when things don't go our way. We can model a life of restoration to our children as we confess our selfishness from a long day and reconcile our relationships. We can trust that our toddler's tantrums are being used for our own transformation into Christlikeness. We can worship and thank God for Christ our hero, who has tethered the dragon, holding him on a leash until Christ's triumphal return.

An Inside-Out Change

I tell my kids, "Speak life." I ask them, "Is what you just said true, necessary, and kind? It must be all three." (Like all my good sayings, I stole it from an older, wiser mother.) It's funny how my ears have built-in radar to hear my children when they idolize something. I hear it in their voices, their choice of words, and the way they interact with others around them. I cringe when I hear their misplaced worship, yet I'm often immune to my own wayward heart, offering myself a free pass to behave and say anything I feel—even when it is anything but life.

When motherhood feels hard, I often want to blame my circumstances, children, or husband. But my biggest problem with motherhood is myself. When I worry about tomorrow's schedule or get frustrated because my morning alone time is short, my heart is revealing what is already there: misplaced worship of my own comforts and control. Can you relate?

So how do we change our heart attitudes? How do we stop feeling as if

---

[6] Revelation 20:10.

[7] Revelation 21:1-4.

controlling our temper, worry, or anxiety is impossible? Contrary to the world's message, our change doesn't happen by working to improve our outside circumstances. The change occurs from the inside out. Instead of strong-arming the world around us, we can stop and ask ourselves, "Am I trusting in God and his promises right now, or am I letting my circumstances fuel my emotions?" By placing our joy, trust, and hope in Christ rather than our situation, our hearts will have a solid, unwavering foundation to rest in regardless of our ever-changing environment.

This sounds like a simple thing, yet at times it feels difficult. But we do this by knowing God's promises and believing in them. And we do that by studying God's Word, spending time in prayer, confessing our sins (even to our youngest children), and preaching the gospel to ourselves.[8] It's bringing our fears, doubts, problems, and cares to the cross. It's trusting that God can handle them better than we can. Believing God's goodness never fails. It's knowing that he is in control and we are not—and believing that's a good thing.

A New Creation

Many of us fear that our negative heart attitudes reflect who we truly are on the inside. We name ourselves: "I am the angry mom, the worrier, the stressed-out mom…" And without Christ, it's true. We are all sinners on a path to self-destruction. Our hearts truly are crooked and erratic, fickle about satisfaction, and headstrong against repentance. We have temperamental hearts with a natural bent toward negative attitudes.

But if you are a believer, you have union with Christ.[9] This means Christ is in you. It is not Christ plus you, or Christ and then you, or Christ and not you. It is Christ *in* you, which means you have everything your warrior, dragon-slaying hero has. When you are stripped bare, when you peel away everything you believe defines you—your hobbies, dreams, skill sets, personality, weaknesses,

---

[8] See chapter 19 for more instruction on how to preach the gospel to yourself.

[9] John 17:23; 1 Corinthians 1:30; 2 Corinthians 13:5.

and sinful tendencies—who are you? If you are in Christ, then it is not the sinful, uncontrollable woman you fear who remains—it is Christ. It is our loving, kind, gracious, merciful Savior in you.

Through your faith in Jesus, you are a new creation in Christ, which means by the power of the Holy Spirit, you can change. You no longer have to give in to temptations, fight for control in all areas of life, or give in to expressing every feeling you have. You are not a victim to your circumstances. Trust that because of Christ's work on the cross, you can grow, improve, and be transformed to be more like him.

Mom, God has not left you to battle the dragon alone. Trust in the promises of God. Believe you are united with Christ. Exchange your worries, fears, and anger with the worship of our good and loving Father who sent his Son to battle on your behalf. Remember that nothing is meaningless in the Christian life. God uses wayward circumstances to reveal the waywardness of our hearts. Each day, as you feel the pressure mounting, the accusations accumulating, the temptations luring, look to Christ to be all you need. He is strong where you are weak. He is perfect where you fail. He is your fullness when you are empty.

He slays the dragon when you need a hero.

DISCUSSION QUESTIONS

1. How do you react when things don't go your way? How does your response reflect what you worship?

2. In what ways do you try to control life by managing your outside environment? How can you submit your desire for control to God? Where can you redirect your hope?

3. What is one area where you can choose to place your joy in Christ and not in your ever-changing environment? What specific steps can you take today to change?

THE GOSPEL
AND OUR TRANSITIONS

Emily

Huge stacks of boxes and clear tubs lined our living room walls, enticing our four young children to arrange them into forts and tunnels. It was a good day if I kept them from unpacking half the toys, books, and kitchen utensils I'd already put away. We were moving, and it couldn't come fast enough.

Even though we were focused on our new home, I was distracted by other things too. A nauseating first trimester meant afternoons on the couch, choking down any food that sounded appetizing. We were in the thick of understanding our 18-month-old son's developmental delays, a painful journey we never planned for. And it was the middle of winter, my least favorite time of the year.

All in all, I wanted all the transitions to end because I couldn't see the good in this exhausting season. If life was going to feel so hard, it needed to matter.

We unloaded the moving truck on a record-high-temperature day in February, and I distinctly remember the sun shining. For a few hours, I stood in our new home flooded with light, and I pictured the end of this season. The thought of unloading boxes and settling in put a smile on my face. The greater hardships of life weren't over, but spring would come. The ice melting off the roof was proof, and I looked forward to the other side of this transition, when the new leaves would sprout and the cornfields around us would yield a harvest.

This wasn't the first life transition I wished away. The long wait between childhood and young adulthood included the awkwardness of adolescence. Between college and career lay a no-man's-land of a million options. The months between dating and engagement were consumed by a season of wondering. Intense pain and pressure stood between the start of labor and the baby in my arms.

From my human perspective, transitions aren't desirable. Instead they're often marked by pain, discomfort, awkwardness, false starts, and conflict. Transitions can feel like a pointless season sandwiched between the good old days and life's next good thing. But we must get from point A to point B, and the in-between is where God does some of his best work of making us more like Christ.

Culture's Message: Find Beauty in the Mess and Look Ahead

In an age of public sharing, we see people lament life's transitions. Moms post pictures of the moving boxes or the progression of their baby bumps with coordinated letter boards. They write about the sadness of the empty womb or express their struggle as they wait for a child's diagnosis. We're getting used to embracing the awkward and painful transitions of life by locking arms and coming alongside one another in the journey.

There is some good in this trend. Acknowledging and validating the messy seasons of life assures us we're not alone. This gives us a sigh of relief. Jesus wept with the hurting, cautious not to gloss over the hardship of struggle, pain, and death. But we have to wonder if positive affirmations and prompts to "look ahead" extend our gaze far enough for real hope.

Lamentations in modern mom culture encourage us to find beauty in the mess. Influencers tell us we'll gain endurance when we verbalize the good around us with gratitude: "Just be positive. You might be having a hard time getting back on your feet and finding joy after baby, but try to enjoy it anyway— you'll cherish these years someday."

We're tempted to look forward to what's next, fixing our eyes on the prize—the end of the transition. We tell ourselves "This pregnancy is hard, but it will all be better when the baby gets here" or "Moving with a toddler feels chaotic, but we're almost to our forever home. Then we'll be settled."

But what happens if the pregnancy doesn't produce a healthy baby? What happens when the child has a medical issue and never sleeps through the night? What happens when the house sale falls through or your husband loses his job? Rooting our hope in our circumstances is always dangerous. So is thinking, "This is my last transition. Once this is over, we'll finally be happy."

Gratitude and positive thinking in the moment is helpful, but it doesn't overshadow all the pain. Looking forward to future events (outside of God's promises) gives relief when things turn out as we hope, but they don't come with a guarantee. We need something that makes all of this worth it, giving us life when things feel like death, providing purpose when our days seem pointless, acknowledging wounds while providing an infinitely better word for our difficult seasons. As hard as it is to remember, we endure for the hope set before us, trusting that God has a greater purpose than the struggle we see today.

The Gospel Message

CREATION: First Eden

When we think about our transitions—from one house to another, from one country to another, from one family size to another, from one era of life to another—we must think about the greater transition of God's people. This journey finds its origins in Eden.

The starting point for mankind was a garden where they had access to God, enjoying fellowship with him.[1] Naked, unashamed, unblemished, commissioned—their work was important. Even though they experienced transitions (imagine Adam and Eve's first day together!), they were uninterrupted by the

---

[1] Genesis 3:8.

frustrating type of exhaustion that marks many of our transitions today. God called all of this very good.[2]

FALL: Banished from Eden

Adam and Eve experienced their first sin-riddled transition when they ate from the tree of the knowledge of good and evil, the one tree God declared off-limits. The "very good" image-bearers went into hiding as shame-filled sinners. The changes and curses would not end there.

Things would be hard for them after the garden—man would toil and struggle in his work, and women would have terrible pain in childbearing.[3] Satan would stick his serpent's hiss into every facet of human life, making even the simplest transitions arduous and hard to bear with faith.

Thousands of years later, modern moms still face their pregnancy trimesters with apprehension and postpartum months with weariness. We are so aware that transition will hold hardship, it's an expectation rather than just a possibility. Going from two kids to three, moving to another country to become missionaries, adjusting to normal family life after a week of vacation, or welcoming another foster child into the home—these things are difficult, just as we predicted. We know we're not in Eden anymore, and we're longing to find a peaceful, beautiful destination that resembles it.

REDEMPTION: Access to Eden

God's people experienced hard transitions after leaving the garden too. Israel, once well provided for under Joseph's care, became slaves longing for rescue. When rescued, they wandered in the desert until they doubted they would reach their destination, the Promised Land. Once they arrived, they endured a series of faithless judges and kings. After the deportation and partial exile, God took them through a long season of prophetic silence as they waited for a Messiah.

God's plan for redemption felt painfully slow, but he was working for

---

[2] Genesis 1:31.

[3] Genesis 3:14-19.

GOD HAS
A GREATER
PURPOSE
THAN THE
STRUGGLE
WE SEE TODAY

restoration in times of transition with a beautiful purpose in mind. Over millennia, he brought history to a point of readiness for his Son's arrival in Bethle-
hem. People were looking for a clear end to their hardship, but God provided
an unexpected solution through his Son, which transitioned his people from
the Old to the New Covenant.[4]

With the help of the indwelling Holy Spirit, God's New Covenant people
could endure trials with joy, knowing they produced a deeper, greater, firmer
faith than before.[5] Believers transitioned from their old self to their new self in
Christ, living holy lives amid challenges.[6] Now we can see ourselves growing
into greater holiness as we behold Christ in our transitions, putting away sin
and loving others as God produces the fruit of the Spirit in us.[7]

Because of Jesus, transitions aren't just marked by pain, difficulty, and struggle—they are part of a redemptive plan, marked by the sanctification of God's
people as they put away old sins and grow in Christlikeness.

CONSUMMATION: A New Eden

All God's New Covenant people are changing while still waiting. We're still
between point A (this season on Earth, where we're already redeemed but not
fully restored) and point B (where Jesus renews all things). Although we experience redemption in smaller seasons of pain, awkwardness, struggle, and refining, these mini-journeys mirror the greater one that ends in the brightest burst
of spring we can imagine.

The guarantee is this: We will make it home.[8] We'll gain perspective about
the trials of this life when we reach the new and better Eden, in full fellowship
with God through Christ forever.

---

[4] Hebrews 8:13.

[5] James 1:2-3.

[6] Ephesians 4:22-23.

[7] 2 Corinthians 3:18; Galatians 5:22-23.

[8] John 6:37.

No Throwaway Seasons

Knowing there is a bigger story that explains the pain and struggle behind life's transitions helps, but honestly, it doesn't always take the edge off when we're not sure if our husband is going to find a new job or we feel like we'll never find a church community in our new town. When we're wrestling through the adjustment of adding an adopted child to the family or we're fretting about the first few weeks of summer break after our kids have been in school all year, we start to feel like this is a throwaway season and our goal is merely to survive.

I can relate to hard seasons of transition when our family size changes. When we had four kids three and under, one being a newborn, the days were incredibly long. One morning before church, my husband left early, leaving me at home with everyone else. I was determined to make food for a potluck we were attending after church. In a couple of hours, I needed to nurse, shower, change everyone's clothes, and make a meal. There was much weeping and gnashing of teeth.

When we finally made it to the potluck, I was so tired and frazzled, I misstepped and dropped the meal before placing it on the table. Seeing the dish shatter into hundreds of shards of glass on the concrete was an embarrassing representation of my heart during our transition to a new normal. I was a big, hot mess going a hundred directions, unsure of my usefulness in such a pitiful state.

Transitions are like that. They can bring out the worst in us, depriving us of what we think we must have to be happy, comfortable, and thriving until our true nature is revealed. God shows us our impatient exasperation when our husband works late every night or travels for weeks on end. He shows us our fickle hearts when a chorus of commotion from our children sends us to seek refuge in social media.

When a goldsmith wants to purify gold, he heats it until the impurities are revealed so he can skim them off. Without the heat, the impurities stay embedded in the gold. Similarly, our circumstances turn up the heat until we see what's in our hearts. It's not that we used to be nice, energetic people, and now (due to this transition and things outside of our control) we're suddenly irritable and unkind. Those changes simply expose the hidden sin that existed all along in the ease and familiarity of our old circumstances.

In the same way, God allows us to experience the pain, difficulty, and discomfort of transitional seasons so our faith is tested and purified because this results in eternal glory and praise for Christ.[9] The transition you just want to end isn't a throwaway season—it's a time full of God's purposes, when hindsight will tell a story of sin and need driving us to the Father and making us love more like the Son.

A Better Thing to Look Forward To

We're right to look forward to something better, but we're often wrong about what that is. We don't just need to hang on until the end of this transition—until we're sleeping through the night again, until we're more familiar with the school routine, or until we unpack our moving boxes. Rather, we need to hang on until we meet Jesus face to face, finding joy and purpose in the meantime.

In the tale *The Pilgrim's Progress*, an allegory of the Christian life, the main character, Christian, goes on a journey from the City of Destruction to the Celestial City.[10] Along the way, he meets trials of various kinds—people who try to persuade him to stray from the narrow path, people who try to satisfy him with worldly pleasures, creatures who try to imprison and defeat him with lies and despair. Each trial is followed by a period of rest or refreshment. He experiences the joy of encouragement and fellowship with other believers, but he nearly drowns on the last leg of the journey as he crosses the river to the Celestial City.

Stories like this remind us that our goal in life is not simply to survive this current hard thing in hopes that it will be our last. Rather, we endure whatever God has for us to the very end, believing God's promises even when we can't see the outcome.

God doesn't promise our current hard season or transition will end the way

---

[9] 1 Peter 1:7.

[10] John Bunyan, *The Pilgrim's Progress* (Chicago, IL: Moody, 2007).

GOD HAS
GOOD
PURPOSES
FOR TODAY

we want it to, but he does promise he'll be with us all the way through it. He'll provide strength, refreshment, and encouragement until we reach our final point B, where we'll never experience sorrow again.[11] Just as he provided an oasis for the tired, thirsty Israelites on their journey in the desert, he can provide refreshment in our transitional times when we cry out to him in faith.[12]

In my season of morning sickness, young children, moving boxes, and medical concerns, I needed a promise of spring. But it wasn't just that flowers would bloom and corn would grow when we finally moved into our house (things stayed in boxes for much longer than I hoped). Or that I would be full of energy in that second trimester (I was actually tired the whole way through the pregnancy). Or that my son would progress and pull out of his medical issues (he didn't, and our concerns grew). I needed to see the value in the season of transition, when God was shoveling, tilling, raking—messing up the hard soil of my heart. He was ready to plant new seeds of faith that could later produce a great harvest for the kingdom. He was not content to let the field of my life stay dormant.

The ultimate spring we all need to look forward to is the defrosting of Satan's cold grip on this earth, when the full and final sunshine of God and the Lamb lights up the streets of the New Jerusalem.[13] That's the true end to this big, groaning transition we're all in, and it's the only thing we can count on.

Transitional seasons are part of life. We might not enjoy every aspect of them, but we don't have to fear them. God loves us too much to let us be comfortable and unscathed. Adoption, infertility, job loss, sick family members, new careers, and new schools might feel like transitions we don't want to bear. But let's rejoice when we have moments of joy and rest, knowing that God has good purposes for today and a sure promise of our final destination.

---

[11] Psalm 23:4; 2 Corinthians 12:9-10; Revelation 21:4.

[12] Exodus 15:22-27.

[13] Revelation 21:23.

DISCUSSION QUESTIONS

1. What transition are you in right now, and how are you coping with the stress it brings?

2. How might God be working in your transition, making it about more than just survival? What areas of sin and idolatry do you see that you weren't aware of before, and what will you do about them?

3. Knowing this isn't a throwaway season, what will you thank God for today?

THE GOSPEL
AND OUR MARRIAGES

Laura

On my first Valentine's Day dating my husband, he went all out: A line of chocolate candies ending in two dozen roses. A horse-drawn sleigh ride with fur blankets and thermoses of hot chocolate. A fancy dinner out on the town where tiny little boats delivered sushi to our table. Diamond earrings.

Bet you didn't see that last one coming, did you? When he gave them to me, I immediately started crying and told him I didn't deserve them. I had never been so spoiled, so extravagantly celebrated, simply because someone liked me.

Fast-forward to Valentine's Day 2018—ten years of being together, seven years of marriage, and three children later: We just moved and were living temporarily at my parents', so we met up after work to look at a potential property to buy. I carried the baby while he held the hands of the older two as we tromped through the snow to survey the land. Afterward, we grabbed a bite to eat at a local restaurant filled with couples—we were quite possibly the only people with children in the entire building. While there, we caught our oldest in a lie. I nodded to Daddy to deal with it, and he did. But I found it insufficient and couldn't resist adding my two cents to drive home the "grievousness of falsehoods" to my four-year-old, who had already zoned out.

When we got home, we divided duties. I took the baby for a bottle, he took the toddlers to wash their hands and brush their teeth. Eventually, we all ended up in the same room together. My husband turned on some music, and immediately a full-family dance party began. Once all the kids were down, my husband slid a chocolate heart covered in red foil across the kitchen counter to me and said, "Happy Valentine's Day, babe. Look what I got you—it was free from work."

Things have changed a little, to say the least. While our first Valentine's Day will always hold a special place in my heart (and not just because of its extravagance), I love the way the holiday has changed for us. Not only in where we live, what our family looks like, and how we spend our days—I love the way *I've* changed. My husband and I are incredibly different from one another, and God has used marriage and raising children to put me through the refiner's fire. The chafe of sanctification hurts—sometimes so much I can hardly stand it— but I am thankful for the work God has done to grow me in holiness. I still have a long way to go (like my pointless need for control during a discipline moment), but God is using my husband to help me remove the dross until only the gold remains.

Culture's Message: Easy, Breezy Love

I was recently at a double bridal shower, and as I listened to the engaged women talk about their upcoming weddings, I couldn't help but think back to mine. I was like them, so full of hope and optimism. Their relationships with their fiancés bursting with romance, compromise, communication!

As brides prepare to walk down the aisle, they're often filled with confidence: "As long as we have each other, we're going to be okay, no matter what life throws at us!" The world tells us marriage will be roses, sleigh rides, diamonds, and boats that bring you sushi for dinner. We are worthy of an easy love, the kind with romance all day and snuggles all night. A marriage of excitement, fulfillment, and unrestrained passion! While we know there will be hard things in the future, many of us believe all the problems are "out there," and we'll face them with our husbands as they come.

But quickly the jig is up. Like a volcano, the infatuation of love erupts with passion and then burns out, leaving you knee-deep in gray ash to clean up. Your husband fails you, you fail him, and your confidence in marriage is shaken. Suddenly your problems are not "out there"—they're in the house, living *with* you and (though you may not see it yet) *inside* you. But don't worry—culture has another answer, transitioning from "Marriage will make you happy!" to "Your children will make you happy!"

The next thing you know, you're looking for fulfillment in the tiny, crying baby you just swaddled like an egg roll in the crib. Your knight in shining armor is now the enemy as you whisper-yell in the middle of the night, angry with one another about something neither of you can control. As your children grow, so do your grievances against your husband. Our inner protective nature soothes our hurting souls by blaming Dad for the relational strain and strife. So you tally up all the ways your husband has failed, build a wall of protection, and hold him at arm's reach—but draw those babies close.

It's a vicious cycle. One that won't end unless one of you waves the white flag and admits, "I'm the problem. I'm sorry—will you forgive me?" But this is not done easily. We might be able to eke out a surface-level apology and do a bit of behavior modification on our own strength, but we'll never be able to truly change our outward behavior unless we dig deeper for a modification of the heart. And transformation at that level comes only from the refining, reconstructive work of the gospel.

The Gospel Message

CREATION: One Union

Much like the brides at the bridal shower I went to, the first bride and groom probably began their marriage with unveiled hope and optimism. When God brought Eve to Adam for the first time, it was the first of countless wedding ceremonies that would bring two dewy-eyed people together for a lifetime.[1] God gave the new couple purpose and a mission—to be fruitful and multiply and to keep order on the earth.[2] Imaging God in unique ways, they were different from one another, but their differences were not divisive—they were assets. They needed one another to complete the tasks given to them by God. In Eden they were unified, two becoming one, as they selflessly worked together, living out a beautiful picture of love and harmony through worship of God alone.

FALL: A Divided Union

Yet as in our own marriages, Adam and Eve were not immune to each other's failures. Just three short chapters into the Bible, their perfect relationship is a thing of the past. When Eve doubted God had a good design for her life and union with Adam, sin and division entered the world, slicing right through the marriage relationship.

Now, as husband and wife, instead of being united as God designed, we sometimes live as two individuals sitting on different sides of the table. We act as enemies, not allies. The sole judge and jury of the other's ability to live out right purpose and mission. We set our own standards rather than accepting God's. Both seek the upper hand, and instead of out-loving one another, we look to marriage to fulfill our own self-serving needs and desires. Sin and its pain make us afraid to be open, honest, and vulnerable. As mothers, we are tempted to hide behind our children, granting them unconditional love while holding our husbands to an ever-growing list of unattainable conditions.

In marriage, we sometimes live as "I" rather than "we" because "we" can feel too risky. It's too painful, too hard, too vulnerable. We do not want a union because we do not want to die to self.

REDEMPTION: Unified in Christ

In our sinful state, we never could have died to ourselves anyway, but

---

[1] Genesis 2:24.

[2] Genesis 1:28.

thankfully, Christ made a way. Jesus loved us more than any earthly husband ever could, living a perfect life and purchasing our union with him at the highest price: his very life. Through his sacrifice, he fully displayed what marriage only shadows—the covenant love between God and his people.[3] This love paved a way so we *could* die to ourselves. This happened once when we were justified before the throne. Then it's played out over and over again through sanctification as we daily deny our old nature, take up our cross, and follow him.[4]

Through Jesus' death, our severed union with God is healed, and we are one in Christ. Being "in Christ" is good news for our marriages because as believers, we now share in Christ's wonderful inheritance from the Father. This means we have in us the very same love he has—a love more true and wonderful than any fairy tale or romantic comedy ever created.[5] Jesus' love is what motivated him to be patient with needy people, kind to those who hurt him, and long-suffering with those who didn't follow his instructions. His love propelled his compassion with the hurting, his offer of grace to sin-filled hearts, and his endless forgiveness when he was rejected, maligned, and scorned. His love took him all the way to death on the cross for us.

In Christ, this is the same love a wife can have for her husband.

CONSUMMATION: Unified Forever

Someday, the experience of our union with Christ won't be blurred by the messiness of this cursed earth. When Christ our King returns to bring us, his bride, physically to himself, we'll no longer have to fight our sinful desires. We won't experience marriage in heaven as we know it today,[6] but we will get to enjoy the best and truest marriage there is: marriage with Christ himself. And there, we'll also image the beautiful relationship with our fellow saints that Adam and Eve enjoyed with one another before the fall.

---

[3] Ephesians 5:23.

[4] Mark 8:34.

[5] Romans 8:17.

[6] Luke 20:27-36.

This means we'll have no more pointless, late-night arguments about how to get the baby to sleep, no more heated whispers in the car about a discipline issue, no more accusations of "You did, you didn't, you don't understand." In consummation, we will experience perfect relationship, fellowship, and union with other believers because of the wondrous, sacrificial love of our bridegroom.

The Pressure for Perfection

One day I'll be in awe of my husband, looking at him in adoration as he drives our minivan. The next day, possibly in that very same minivan, I'm thinking about all the ways he could improve as a husband and a father. Maybe I recently listened to a podcast on parenting, and I couldn't help but think about how much he needed to hear it. Or maybe a friend shared how her husband structures morning quiet times as a family, and now I'm finding my husband's bedtime readings insufficient.

In turn, I might make a disapproving remark about how there's some dust on his Bible, or perhaps I'll follow up his discipline talk with one of my own because I find his wanting. Maybe I'll say nothing at all as I quietly build a wall between us, brick by brick.

I'm willing to bet I'm not alone in holding up a standard for what an "involved Christian dad" looks like—a standard of my own creation rather than God's.

In the Old Testament, God lays out part of his plan for parents raising children, and it's surprisingly uncomplicated. He charges parents to intentionally invest in their children and teach them to love God and his laws.[7] They are to be diligent in this and do it all the time. For us today, that means weaving the gospel into the life we're already living. It doesn't tell us that carrying out this command has to include a 20-minute family quiet time with Dad on the guitar, leading the children in worship. It just says to do it, however that looks. Even though faithfulness to that end can be hard, we are the ones overcomplicating it.

---

[7] Deuteronomy 6:4-9.

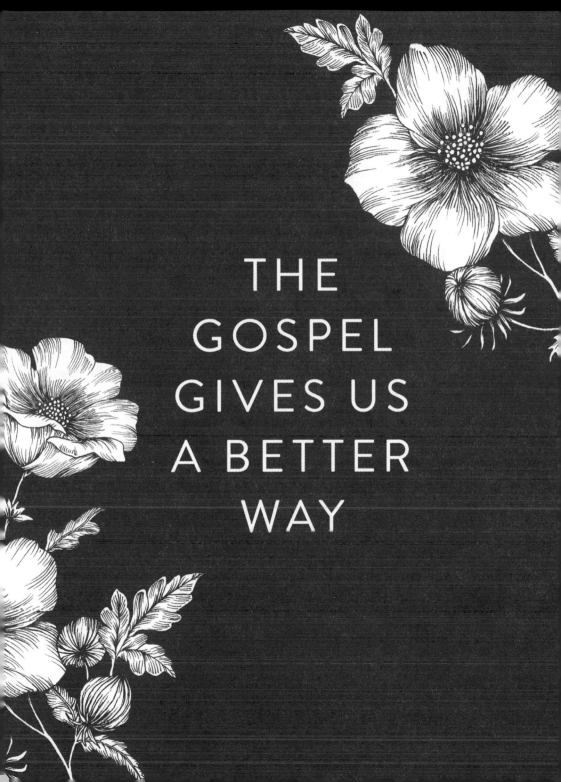

THE
GOSPEL
GIVES US
A BETTER
WAY

The beautiful thing about God creating us as parents with unique personalities, strengths, and gifts is that we can live out our differences while still having unity in our marriage relationship. Your husband doesn't need to invest in your children in the same ways you would—or the same way that Instagram dad you're following does. In fact, because God made man and woman to display himself uniquely, you're better parents together than alone, balancing out one another's strengths and weaknesses as you strive to live out the gospel in your own home.

Here's some good news: Because Jesus lived a perfect life in our stead, the pressure is off for both husband and wife to execute perfect parenting. Jesus never missed a teaching moment, he never misspoke or made a theological error, he never had impure motives or an impatient attitude, and he never failed the people around him. He lived a perfect life, and because we have union in Christ, we can trust him with what we have to offer as parents of our children. And if you're both believers, you each have the gift of the Holy Spirit to help you grow in parenting, maturity, and your understanding of God's design for the family.

Mom, Christ has measured up on your behalf. Now you can stop comparing your husband to the parenting books, the conferences, the bloggers, or the next-door neighbor. Instead, offer your husband the relentless grace and love you've received from your shared inheritance with Christ, celebrating the unique ways your husband is gifted. You can be brave enough to risk the areas where your heart is broken and worn thin in marriage, trusting God to draw your family to himself despite human flaws and failures.

The Road of Grace

Perhaps as you read this, your heart is heavy. Maybe your husband isn't a believer, or maybe he's so checked out, you're not sure where he's at in his walk with the Lord. Yet even if your husband is striving to faithfully live out God's calling for fathers, there is still sin, there is still failure. We all have flaws this side of eternity. Often as wives, our first response is to disrespect our husbands, to nag, grumble, manipulate, worry, and rant.

But the gospel gives us a better way. No matter where you're at with your husband, let him see the work of Christ in you. Remember, when you were still dead and stuck in your sin, Jesus loved you so much he died for you.[8] Offer that same love to your husband. Rather than looking at everything he's doing wrong, begin finding everything he's doing right. Let Christ's love in you be stronger than any misunderstanding, bigger than any feelings of resentment, louder than your desire for justice, and greater than your own prideful heart.

Marriage may sometimes feel like sandpaper for our souls, but the rough strokes shape and mold us to be more like the image of God. In our marriages, let's be the first to respond with kindness, to speak with gentleness, to be understanding, accommodating, and self-sacrificing. If you're like me, it's easy to forget that we cannot bring the conviction of the Holy Spirit to our husbands. Instead we can pray for them, asking God to intervene and give us peace and trust in the process. Instead of crushing our husbands with our words, let's crush the thoughts of comparison that run so easily through our minds. Instead of focusing on our husbands' flaws or ignoring them completely and focusing only on our children, let's stay focused on our own relationship with Christ.

Mom, let's be advocates, supporters, champions of unity, and our husbands' biggest fans. Marriage may not be what we thought it was when we first walked down that aisle. But because Christ loved us first, we can overflow with the extravagant love of Christ for our husbands, unveiling a love deeper and more transcendent and brilliant than we could have ever predicted.

> *This chapter mainly addresses offenses, heartaches, and tensions that commonly arise from sin within marriage. However, if abuse (physical, emotional, or sexual) or other illegal or illicit behavior is occurring in your marriage, please tell someone and reach out for counsel and professional intervention.*

---

[8] Romans 5:6-8.

YOU'RE BETTER PARENTS TOGETHER THAN ALONE

DISCUSSION QUESTIONS

1. Do you impose any standards on your husband for what an involved Christian dad looks like? How do your standards compare with God's?

2. Christ loved us so much, he gave up his life for ours. In what ways should Christ's sacrificial love motivate your own love toward your husband?

3. What are some things you can prayerfully work on in the way you view and interact with your husband?

THE GOSPEL AND
OUR MUNDANE MOMENTS

Emily

Hey, babe! Come over here. You've *got* to see this." After tucking a shirt into a drawer, I leaned over his shoulder to see what was pulled up on the iPad.

"Here, just watch this." He handed it to me with a grin. After a season of research on minimalist living, I had some idea of what I might see.

A family appeared in the video. Six or seven children were smiling and leading the way to a laundry room turned "family closet." Stacks of labeled baskets lined the walls, each assigned to a different child. The mom explained their "bundle system," showing how she matched outfits on the counter, rolling them up like a sushi chef and enclosing them with thick rubber bands. I looked down to see my husband's smile.

"Well, what do you think?" He was fascinated and hopeful he'd found a way to eradicate our laundry piles.

After watching the video, we pulled out all the kids' clothes, wrapping outfit bundles of our own. Weeks went by as our hope in the new system peaked—and dwindled. The laundry bundles made it easier to select outfits (especially for our twins) and helped us decrease the quantity of clothing in use. But there was a catch. Crafting clothing bundles added significant time to the folding process.

We had to wait for all loads to be clean at the same time so we could match outfits and spend our evenings marathon-rolling.

We tried other ways to ease the laundry burden too: KonMari folding, capsule wardrobes, a five-outfit limit for each child, wearing pants or pajamas several days in a row, and more. Each of these methods added a hopeful new efficiency, but it also added a new cumbersome step. No matter what we tried, the reality remained: Laundry for a family of seven takes time.

Our history of laundry management reveals an underlying theme: a couple on a quest to escape the doldrums of everyday life. We wanted to make things orderly—not always for the glory of God but to minimize our ordinary workload and have more time for something extraordinary. Something that *really* matters. Not laundry. That's boring.

Culture's Message: Extraordinary Is Better Than Mundane

As moms, we often feel trapped by the less exciting aspects of life. We bristle as we rearrange the wooden train tracks for the hundredth time and pick up the same dirty tennis shoes over and over. We sigh as we hunt for the missing pacifier under the couch and have the same conversation about boundaries hour after hour. This is the very essence of the mundane—the monotonous, wearisome moments that feel devoid of meaning. The run-of-the-mill stuff you must do because you're a mom and you're responsible for these little people.

But the world around us primarily values visible gains. It doesn't affirm ordinary faithfulness—the wiped counters, the clean diapers, the stacks of well-loved books. Burdened by the mundane, we wonder if we need to spend our time in better ways. Maybe if our moments were more interesting and meaningful, all our work would finally matter. We wonder, "Is this all there is?"

Feelings of stasis cause us to tally our mundane moments until we deserve something more exciting like a vacation, a visit to the salon, a night with our girlfriends, a splurge at the store, or some time on the couch. "I've taken care of the kids and the house, so I'm going to head out for a few hours with my girlfriends!" We hint to our husbands about the need for a nice card or a big bouquet of flowers. We post pictures of everyday life to garner likes on social media. This way, when people see our folded laundry bundles, they can affirm our hard work.

If we can't add up our mundane investments to earn something better, we might try to gain control of them with the latest and greatest strategies. "Minimalist living" videos, organizational blogs, and thoughtful podcast episodes offer us hope for defeating the never-ending cycle of responsibilities that accompany family life. If we can't eliminate the mundane, we can at least subdue it for our purposes.

Finding meaning in the mundane is a good goal, but when meaning means adventures, accomplishments, and accolades, we might have missed the point. We can try to flee the mundane and replace it with something better. We can pick up a hobby, invest in new relationships, and try to make the most of our time for a little more productivity and joy in life under the sun. But despite our efforts, we're still left wondering if we've done enough for it to really matter, as every fresh thing eventually becomes ordinary.

If motherhood is mostly lived one mundane moment to the next and the mundane moments don't live up to our world-changing expectations—if we feel like we can't get ahead and live an extraordinary life—then really, what's the point? Can the gospel help us have purpose and joy and see God's extraordinary work amid laundry mountains, rocking chairs, work commutes, sinks full of dishes, and long mornings of playtime with our children?

The Gospel Message

CREATION: Good, Ordinary Work for God's People

In the beginning, God meant for his people to work, and much of their work was to be both good and mundane. From our vantage point, it seems like naming the animals was an extraordinary job—but likely, this was just Adam's day-in and day-out responsibility, given to him for worship, purpose, and enjoyment.[1] As Adam and his helper, Eve, brought order to God's earth with goodness, thoughtfulness, and authority, they imaged God and brought him glory. There was dignity in their everyday lives because their work found its origins in God's command.

As mothers, we continue to reflect God's character in each moment as we conform to his likeness. Ordinary moments existed before the fall, and they were not demeaned or dismissed by God. Instead they were good and valuable for the flourishing of life.

FALL: Ordinary People Wanting to Be like Their Extraordinary God

Unfortunately, Eve wasn't satisfied with the fullness of God's provision in Eden or the knowledge and responsibilities he'd given her. Instead she listened to the serpent, who tempted her to seek the extraordinary—becoming like God himself by eating from the tree of the knowledge of good and evil.[2] She was the first human who wanted to step outside the ordinary, human, limited bounds of God's commands into something greater, godlike, and unlimited.

This spills over into our lives when we're tempted to believe that ditching today's mundane need to change the diapers, discipline the children, feed the hungry, answer the emails, wash the dishes, pay the bills, and so on is frivolous work that is somehow beneath us. Instead of accepting the good boundaries and responsibilities God has given us, we long to throw them off and play god, giving ourselves control over different and supposedly better things. Like Eve, we want to do God's job, especially if it means forgoing the less exciting moments of life.

We've stopped finding our identity in who we are (image-bearers of God) and started trying to find it in what we can do (having "open eyes" and hoping to be wise).[3] We want more fancy and less normal. We want more fine dining and less peanut butter and jelly.

---

[1] Genesis 2:15,19.

[2] Genesis 3:5.

[3] Genesis 3:6.

But when we rank the value of our lives on productivity, comparing external circumstances to see who's doing the best and most interesting stuff, we'll never be content with our day-to-day lives. As long as we pride ourselves in our ability to speed through normalcy so we can get on to the better parts of life, we're walking in Eve's faithless footsteps.

REDEMPTION: Christ's Ordinary Life and Extraordinary Love

God knew that once his relationship with his people was severed, there would be no way back without an incredible intervention. Jesus' life was a paradox of ordinary and extraordinary. He entered the world through the everyday pattern of childbirth through the miraculous means of a virgin's womb.[4] He lived a mundane childhood of working, eating, playing, and learning—one so normal that we have little to no record of it, although we know it was without sin.[5]

Before Jesus' public ministry, he spent more than a decade engaged in a normal vocation. In his public ministry, he continued to do mundane things, like spending time with his disciples, having meals with people, teaching day after day, and traveling. But although he had a taste of mundane life, he lived it extraordinarily—as only the incarnate God could do. He performed miracles, forgave sin, calmed storms, healed the sick, and raised people from the dead.

His most extraordinary task culminated as God accomplished the salvation of his people through crucifixion, a death sentence endured by common criminals. God works in both the ugly and the mundane to bring new life, redemption, and his sovereign plan to fruition, and such is the same for those indwelled with the Holy Spirit.

With the Holy Spirit as our Helper, we can now reframe, appreciate, and utilize our most mundane moments as a means of grace for others and ourselves. We don't always know how God works, but we trust him without seeing because

---

[4] Matthew 1:23.

[5] 2 Corinthians 5:21.

we believe that he accomplishes his good will even when it looks ordinary to our human eyes.[6] His redemptive plan unfolded through millennia of normal people whose mundane moments came together in victory over death as Jesus left his tomb. He's really the one who plays an extraordinary role in the story.

CONSUMMATION: Ordinary Work Made New

Although we don't have all the details, Scripture tells us that God will make all things new. Like Adam and Eve in Eden, we'll do purposeful, good, even mundane work—all for God's glory. We'll stop ranking the "cool factor" of our work for the sake of our pride, and instead, we'll crown Jesus with many crowns.[7] All the moments of our lives—ordinary and extraordinary—will give us reason to fall before the Lamb on the throne, worshipping his worthiness in all things.

You Never Know What God Is Doing

The story line of the Bible shows that ordinary people didn't always know when God was using their mundane moments, common vocations, everyday relationships, faithful interactions, and continual prayers for his bigger plans and purposes.

In the account of the Exodus, the midwives Shiphrah and Puah did a brave thing when they deceived Pharaoh and saved the Hebrew babies in the context of their ordinary work.[8] Through their faithfulness amid mundane, wearisome, everyday moments—supporting women through labor, bringing babies into the world, helping them nurse and survive—God thwarted Pharaoh's plans to eradicate a generation.

Although Mary experienced a miraculous conception by the Holy Spirit and was the mother to God's own Son, many of her mothering days were probably spent pregnant with other children, nursing them, preparing food for her family,

---

[6] Hebrews 11:1.

[7] Revelation 19:12.

[8] Exodus 1:15-16.

THERE IS NO
MUNDANE MOMENT
TOO SMALL FOR
GOD'S GLORY TO
SHINE THROUGH IT

teaching and training children, gathering water, and so on. God brought up his extraordinary Son, the Redeemer of the world, in an ordinary home.

The reality is, most of the bystanders in the Bible lived ordinary lives. People of faith and their mundane work went undocumented while God did good, glorious things through their lives. This should cause us to take heart.

When I'm rocking a child to sleep for the thousandth night in a row, I can have faith that God can use that everyday moment to bring about his will for our lives. When I'm talking to my children at the breakfast table while someone squeezes too much syrup on their waffles, I can have faith that those conversations plant seeds that I can't see. When I roll laundry bundles, bring in another week's worth of groceries, put the baby's toys in the living room basket, and wipe the table for the umpteenth time, I can remember that I image God as I bring order to my little corner of God's creation. I don't always know how that image communicates the character of God to those around me, but I trust that it does.

I trust that there is no mundane moment too small for God's glory to shine through it.

Mundane Life in Christ

The part of us that wants to accomplish something extraordinary and be "like God" still exists. The part of our heart that longs for more than laundry piles, sitting in the car at the school pick-up line, and dealing with the same issues with the same old coworkers still burns.

I often want to find answers to those longings by manipulating my life to be fresher and more exciting, less normal and run of the mill. I swipe through social media feeds on my phone, hoping to see something interesting to add to my own life. I try to make washing the dishes more interesting by listening to podcasts while I scrub. Being thoughtful with my time is a good thing, but my deepest longing for glory and purpose is found in Christ.

Mom, because we're united to him, our identity *is* extraordinary and our calling *is* magnificent. Remember, we're part of an epic story headed for a glorious ending. We're really not that special, but Christ in us is spectacular. He's our hope for glory.[9] We can do all kinds of extraordinary things with a new nature bought and provided for by him through the Holy Spirit.

It might be mundane to fold laundry, but it's extraordinary to do it patiently with joy and a heart of love. It might be mundane to sit on the couch and read another book to a whiny four-year-old, but it's extraordinary to show kindness and mercy to an undeserving sinner. It might be mundane to fill the fridge with groceries, but it's extraordinary to praise God for his provision. Our everyday moments might be ordinary, but when we accomplish them while displaying the fruit of the Spirit, they reflect our extraordinary Savior.[10]

So the laundry piles will keep coming and coming and coming—and I'm sure my husband will keep trying to find ways to make the process more orderly and efficient. But we can pursue excellence in our hidden, everyday moments, knowing that "to live is Christ."[11] Even folding laundry is "from him and through him and to him."[12] And that isn't mundane at all.

DISCUSSION QUESTIONS

1. What's one of your least favorite mundane activities in motherhood? How would you describe how it makes you feel, and why does it make you feel that way?

2. How does Jesus identify with you in that mundane activity, and how does your role in God's redemptive story give that activity new purpose?

3. How will you show God's character to those around you today or this week as you complete your mundane activity?

---

[9] Colossians 1:27.

[10] Galatians 5:22-23.

[11] Philippians 1:21.

[12] Romans 11:36.

THE GOSPEL AND OUR BIRTH EXPERIENCES

Laura

I was midway through my first pregnancy when I felt the nesting instinct start to kick in. But the instinct was less about preparing for the actual baby and more about preparing for labor and delivery. I had been reading birth stories online and asking friends how their labors went, and I was inspired to plan and prepare for my own dream birthing experience.

I purchased the top-selling labor and delivery books on Amazon, interviewed a few doulas I found online, toured a birthing center that had one of the lowest C-section rates in the state, and enrolled my husband and myself in a local birthing class recommended by a friend who attested what she learned there helped her achieve her "perfect all-natural birth experience." By the time I was 32 weeks, I had a two-page birth plan that included low lighting, a soothing playlist, a long list of preferred comfort techniques, and even the type of IV I would prefer. (A heparin lock, in case you're wondering.)

"I think I can do this, honey. The all-natural labor and delivery is mine if I really want it. Women are warriors! Our bodies were built for this!" I would exclaim something like this to my husband every couple of weeks as I verbally processed how I pictured the way our firstborn would join us. My husband was a trooper, supporting me in my hopes for an all-natural birth (even though he didn't entirely understand my zeal) but also reminding me, "We don't actually know how it will go, right? We're dealing with another life joining the world— it's going to be unpredictable, don't you think?"

"Well, sure," I'd reply. But deep down, I wasn't so sure. Barring a super-fast delivery, I had a plan. The doctors and hospitals should listen to me, and I want what's best for my baby and me—shouldn't that be enough to get the birth story I want?

At 39 weeks I went into labor. Thirty-six hours later, I held a healthy, seven-pound, four-ounce baby boy in my arms, yet I lay in the delivery bed exhausted, defeated, and disappointed. A copy of my birth plan lay on the floor beside me, crumpled and abandoned, just like my dream birth experience. Instead of over-whelming joy for the new life in my arms, I felt hot, bitter tears run down my cheeks. My son felt foreign in my arms, and I was uncomfortable and awkward, ready to hand him back to my husband.

In the weeks and months that followed, the questions ran through my mind: "What went wrong with my plan? Could we have done something different? Did it have to go that way? Why was my birth story so bad?"

Culture's Message: Perfection Is Possible

From a young age, women are often raised to hope that someday they'll be mommies and birth children of their own. As women, they slowly learn about how it actually works. Close friends describe how contractions feel as they build, sisters reveal the horrors of a peri bottle but try to convince you it's magic, and birth stories shared online recount every detail (through words *and* pictures) of the labor and delivery experience. Internet searches explain what to pack in your hospital bag, how to make a birth plan, and what songs are most soothing during transition. The how-tos and advice to achieve a perfect birth story (whatever "perfect" means to you) are an endless well. Particularly when it's a woman's first time giving birth, she collects and organizes these stories and tips, storing them up like a safety net to ensure the birth of her dreams.

Nowadays, the perfect birth story is sought after like the Holy Grail. If we just read the right books, practice the methods, and have enough stamina and willpower, we have the power to manipulate one of the most vulnerable, undignified things we'll ever do, making it bend to our desires as a display of our own strength and control. Our natural bent toward pride tells us that if we get our perfect birth story, we get to parade it around like a badge of honor. Swapping birth stories at a dinner date or recounting the tale at a baby shower? Make sure you mention you did it just like you planned. The worldly merits of sharing our perfectly controlled and crafted birth stories are alluring. Who doesn't want to sound like a hero?

Some women's experiences do match their plans. But for many women, no matter how much willpower they mustered up in the delivery room, their birth story was anything but what they planned for. It's painful to reach our limits and see our failures. Instead of feeling like a hero, we feel like a zero, so why not act like we didn't care anyway?

So we cover our disappointment and despair for a certain type of birth by making light of it: "We don't actually care that much. Let's have a good laugh about it!" Posting pictures on social media of the messiness and indignities of birth with funny captions, we tell our friends and families with raw honesty and jokes about how no one was with us and we didn't know what to do, how our water broke in public, or how our husband almost fainted because of all the blood in the delivery room. We cover our pain, suffering, and sorrows with humor and lightheartedness—turning an intimate, sensitive experience into a comedy act for dinner-party entertainment.

Each subsequent birth is a new chance to prove yourself, a chance to either show that last time, it wasn't a fluke—you truly are a warrior-goddess—or this time, the underdog finally gets a win.

If not, well, hopefully there will at least be a funny story.

No matter how birth goes, all women agree that labor and delivery is hard. It's unpredictable. It's painful. The curse that fell on Eve is alive and well on every woman who walks this earth, and it is the great leveler of the female race.

It brings out the truth of our human condition: We are helpless and in need of a Savior. It's important to prepare and understand birth to be a good steward of our bodies and our babies, but we are not goddesses with unlimited control over our stories, nor are we immune to the pain and hardship of a birth that doesn't go according to plan.

So we must take our birth plans and stories, no matter how they turn out, and lay them at the cross. We must trust that our hopes and dreams for a perfect birth lie within a greater plan and story—to redeem not only our childbirths but all of creation.

The Gospel Message

CREATION: Be Fruitful and Multiply

"Be fruitful and multiply and fill the earth."[1] That was God's charge to Adam and Eve in the garden soon after he created them. There he blessed them, giving them their instructions for life, which included the command to bear children. Without the fall, labor and delivery would not have been riddled with pain and weakness as we experience them today. Birth stories would have won all the *oohs* and *aahs* at a baby shower and would have been more desirable than any of the most perfect birth experiences we hear about today.

FALL: The Sting of the Curse

"I will surely multiply your pain in childbearing; in pain you shall bring forth children."[2] When Adam and Eve disobeyed God and ate from the forbidden tree in the garden, a curse fell generally on man and woman for their sin and specifically on women and their birth experience. Since then, "be fruitful and multiply" doesn't just mean the great joy of having children. Now it's a phrase mingled with heavy pain, toil, and suffering.

For centuries now, women have intimately felt the weight of the curse when

---

[1] Genesis 1:28.

[2] Genesis 3:16.

it comes to bearing children. In places without modern medicine, childbirth is still a leading cause of death for women. Even today, while there are rumors of med-free, pain-free childbirths, childbirth usually includes moments of intense pain, great weakness, and a sharp awareness of our inabilities. Now we come out of the delivery room with stitches, scars, bruises, and wounds. Many of us are stunned by the way our stories unfolded. For the most grievous of birth stories, the curse of sin and death prevents some women from ever meeting their babies or only allows enjoying them for a short time. And sadly, some women never receive a chance to experience labor and delivery at all.

After the fall, the entire journey of motherhood is wrought with fear, toil, and sacrifice. The pain of bearing children begins the day of conception and continues not just through the birth but beyond, through the toddler years, grade school, graduation day, and a lifetime. We have not only physical pain and hardship but also a wayward heart, constantly seeking control, stability, and safety in anything but God. Particularly in childbirth, we have a mentality of finding comfort and escape from the curse on our physical bodies without thinking about our need to escape the greater curse on our souls. We hope to redeem our birthing experiences rather than trust in our true Redeemer.

REDEMPTION: Deliverance from Delivery

But remarkably, it was through the very thing by which we're cursed that God sent our Savior, who would eventually deliver us. A young girl, alone and outcast, unsure of where or how she would have her baby until the day she went into labor, Mary finally delivered our Redeemer among the animals, dirt, and straw. This was no birthing center. There was no whirlpool tub or aromatherapy, and it's doubtful that Joseph knew what counterpressure was. But it was through a birth story in a tiny town in Israel that God continued writing his Big Story, sending our Redeemer as a baby who would eventually bear the full brunt of the curse on the cross, taking away all our shame, suffering, and trauma and replacing them with hope, peace, and grace.

Jesus came through the curse to break the curse.

Because Christ absorbed the curse, we don't find our hope in a perfectly developed birth plan, we don't trust our bodies to "do what they were made to do," and we don't find our identity in how close we came to a desirable birth experience. Because of Christ's sacrifice, we place our trust in God alone. He is the Creator of life and the only one who can provide true deliverance as we deliver a baby or recover from a birth that didn't go according to our plan.

In these days of modern medicine, God's mercies in our stories run aplenty: hospitals and doctors, doulas and birthing balls, heating and air-conditioning, ultrasound machines, epidurals, necessary medical interventions…the list goes on. These are things that God doesn't have to give us, but because of his love, he does it anyway.

CONSUMMATION: The End of Our Groaning

When our Redeemer returns for good, we'll no longer experience pain through childbirth. On that day, the curse will be fully lifted, every wound will be fully healed, death will rise to life, and we'll be united with our Savior. Today, our outward groaning for redemption from the pains of childbirth mirrors the inward groaning of our hearts for the true redemption that will come with the return of our Savior.[3] Amid our need to control our birth plans, difficulties in labor and delivery, and the feelings of disappointment or pride, we can take hope, knowing our experiences in childbirth are not God's final word for us.

Hope Only in the Gospel Story

You may not have experienced labor and delivery yet, or you might have multiple childbirth experiences, all with different stories and outcomes. But wherever you are with birth, I think many of us feel a natural sense to have some sort of a plan for childbirth. Whether that's walking in and simply knowing you want to ask for the epidural the moment you put on a gown or desiring a home

---

[3] Romans 8:23-24.

JESUS CAME THROUGH THE CURSE TO BREAK THE CURSE

birth with detailed steps for as natural a birth as possible, it's normal to try to prepare and plan for such a huge event in your life.

Of course, being knowledgeable and understanding the process of childbirth and your medical options is wise, but there's a difference between being equipped to make good decisions and needing to be in control of every moment—and then becoming devastated when you're not. Leading up to the birth of my first, I was afraid of the unknown and prideful of my own capabilities. At the heart of it, I didn't trust God to care for me. I worshipped control and worldly perfection, the created rather than the Creator.[4] If you are doing this like I was, it's easy to land in one of two places: pride or despair. Pride and self-worship in your own skills if your story marched to your perfect plan or despair and failure if it all went awry.

Childbirth is a personal and intimate picture of the gospel for a mother.[5] Our response to our birth stories reveals our need for deliverance from a truer, deeper need: our weak and sinful selves. God uses childbearing for sanctification as it acutely and painfully points out how weak we truly are.[6] It reminds us that we are not in control and self-sufficient. We are not, in fact, goddesses.

The tale of our child's birth is unpredictable, but our God is not. From before the beginning of time, our God planned a perfect story of redemption for his people. He has faithfully unfolded it day by day for millennia, and it has impeccably gone to his plan. We live in the story, still with sin, need, weakness, and imperfection, but we can trust our faultless God. He promises to bring his plan to perfection and ultimately deliver us from our sin, uniting us forever with him.

Knowing this, we don't find our hope in the perfect birth story—we find

---

[4] Romans 1:25.

[5] I owe much of my understanding of how childbirth reflects the gospel through the writings of Gloria Furman. Her books *Treasuring Christ When Your Hands Are Full* and *Missional Motherhood* are two great reads on the topic of motherhood.

[6] Romans 8:22-23.

it in our perfect Savior. Jesus Christ, in his deepest, darkest need, when he was weakest and frailest, trusted in God's plan, even to the point of death.

God Writes the Only Perfect Story

As you plan for or reflect on your child's birth, remember that God is the giver of life. He writes the only perfect story. In our birth experiences, God deserves all praise. Amid the decisions, choices, failure, and achievements, we can have a steady, unwavering foundation built on our faithful God and his bigger, perfect story for our lives. He never forsakes us or leaves us to ourselves—he always comes to our aid. It is a mercy that weakness in labor and delivery tears down the barriers we build up and gives us more of what we really need—God himself.

Let's plan for and process our births in a way that worships God, not ourselves. In all of it, trust God and thank him for all he's done and will yet do. As you bear children, consider your new life in Christ and your gratefulness to be a part of his bigger, better—and completely perfect—story.

DISCUSSION QUESTIONS

1. As you reflect on or prepare for an upcoming birth, what are your expectations? Are any of them too idealistic in light of the fall?

2. In what ways does the childbirth process reflect your greater inner needs and weaknesses? How does the gospel meet you with hope?

3. What mercies can you find in your labor and delivery, and how can this cause you to worship?

9

THE GOSPEL AND OUR POSTPARTUM BODY IMAGE

Emily

Before I hit "Post" on Instagram, I hesitated. Less than two weeks after giving birth to our fifth child, I felt self-conscious about my postpartum figure. The handful of happy pictures I'd snapped at my two-year-old's birthday party didn't meet my expectations. Instead of a fresh-looking young mom, I saw someone who looked heavier and more tired than I was comfortable with.

Over the past six years and four pregnancies, I've felt proud when I lost weight quickly, envious when my friends bounced back faster than I did, and ashamed when I couldn't will my stomach flat. With all that baggage in tow, I considered keeping those sweet moments from the birthday party to myself. The part of my heart that desired my own glory worried that the picture revealed the toll childbearing had taken on me, declaring me very ordinary and very human. And even more disconcerting to my sinful heart was the thought that these pictures eroded my claim on external beauty, something I loved to identify with.

As those concerns ran rampant in my heart, the voice of truth grew even louder. I counseled myself with it and replayed the narrative of the gospel. I reminded myself that God wasn't asking me to look as if I'd never had a baby, that worth wasn't tied up in the size of my jeans, and that I wasn't defined by what others thought of me. I am fully righteous before the throne because of grace and through faith. I remembered that this life isn't about me anyway, so I'm free to look how I look and not be caught up in pride or despair.

With that, I decided to hit "Post" after all. This time, I didn't want to be distraught about my postpartum body; I wanted to believe the good news about my standing in Christ and enjoy this season of life. Is that the end of the mental battle for me? No, probably not. But I love the days where lies are displaced by the truth.

Culture's Message: Eliminate All Evidence of Motherhood

The faulty and harmful thinking I rehearsed isn't unique to me; it's often seen in the culture around us. In the age of celebrity and supermodel moms, looking like a regular old mom feels shameful. Aging and weight gain are somewhat taboo and should be countered with serums, personal trainers, and special diets so you can look better than you did at 21. Not only does it feel embarrassing to look postpartum, but it's to your glory to look like you've never had a baby. A gossip blog boasts a "Slimmer Than Before Baby!" headline with a picture of an A-lister on the red carpet, months after giving birth. The normal mom wonders, "How is that possible? What's wrong with my body?"

It's not only "out there" but close to home too. Playdates with friends who complain about their eight-week postpartum body (when they *barely* have a pooch) make us upset and envious. We ask each other for secrets, wondering if breastfeeding or perhaps new control-top leggings are the key. In the closet, our kids poke our tummies and ask when we're having another baby (while the only baby naps in the next room). We can't escape mental questions about our bodies. Even in the bedroom with our husbands, we worry. "Turn off the lights, honey."

Additionally, our culture is slowly shifting from concern about the number on the scale to the worship of a healthy lifestyle. It can seem like those who haven't taken up a fitness regimen after baby, resulting in more defined muscles and a trim figure, don't value themselves or their children. All these messages come wrapped up with a bow and a tag that reads, "There are no excuses. Any mom can do this!"

As stewards of a body created to serve the Lord, we should definitely attend to our health. But the culture sometimes shouts, "Shame on you, Mama. You're not only out of shape; you evidently don't care enough about your kids to model a healthy lifestyle." For an average mom (biologically or through foster care and adoption, which also require sacrifices), anything short of bouncing back to immediate health and a pre-baby weight can feel like a major failure, even if you're faithfully serving your family, staying active, and eating your vegetables.

The Gospel Message

CREATION: Made to Give Life

Let's back up for a minute because God's original design helps us understand what he really thinks about a woman's ability to bear children and the role her body plays in that process.

God created Adam and Eve in the garden in his likeness and without error.[1] Although Eve's body was beautifully designed, her identity wasn't meant to be found in her external appearance. Instead her beauty was meant to glorify God as she worked alongside Adam to accomplish God's commission to be fruitful, multiply, and subdue the earth. Giving birth to children was part of God's original good design.[2]

FALL: Scarred by the Curse

Unfortunately, we won't get to experience the wonderful gift of a perfectly functioning childbearing body. Instead sin entered the picture when Eve doubted God's goodness and disobeyed his clear command in the garden. Sin brought the curse, which not only resulted in the pain and suffering of childbirth but also broke all of creation. Now women would be subject to the realities

---

[1] Genesis 1:26-27.

[2] Genesis 1:28.

of miscarriage, infertility, maternal death, deep stretch marks, issues with weight loss and weight gain, varicose veins, chronic back and pelvic pain, round ligament pain, patchy discolored skin, dark under-eye circles, wrinkles, and more.

Giving life wasn't going to look or feel very life-giving anymore. It was going to be costly, and it would require suffering.

No matter how a woman becomes a mom—biologically or through foster care or adoption—her physical body pays a price. Her time becomes limited, her sleep diminished, her brain filled with the needs of others. Discretionary time decreases as Mom sometimes needs to worry about what her kids will eat before she considers her own meal. But instead of acknowledging a mom's limitations and trusting God's good purposes in them, we often perpetuate the worship of external appearances. Instead of longing for a word about God's work on our character and faithfulness, we long to hear people say, "You look like you didn't even have a baby!" We want to be the mom who didn't have to give up anything to create life. We want it to come free of cost.

REDEMPTION: Identified with a Person, Not a Body Type

But life-giving isn't free. God knew the depths of our capacity for self-worship, so he made a way for our redemption. This wasn't by slapping on a little sin-concealer or fixing our "flawed" postpartum bodies in this life, but by sending his Son to pay the greatest cost for our eternal life. He spiritually restores us for his purposes.

Jesus certainly understands what it means to be scarred, stretched, and marred, even shedding blood so he could give life to others.[3] And after he rose from the dead, he showed those scars to many as a testimony of God's work through his obedience. When we trust in his death on our behalf, we believe we died that death with him and are raised to live a new life in the Spirit.[4] This means we are not pursuing a certain physical appearance in this life. Instead

---

[3] Isaiah 52:14.

[4] Romans 6:4.

LIFE-GIVING
ISN'T FREE

we are pursuing a person who loves us deeply and gives us immeasurable and unchanging worth. The only thing that will make us truly happy isn't a smaller pant size or a six-pack after baby, but Christ himself.

Does this mean that we don't care what happens to our bodies? That we treat them poorly, doing whatever we want, thinking they don't matter at all? By no means! We were purchased by a costly sacrifice, and the very scars Christ carries on his body remind us that we are not our own, but are meant for testifying to God's glory. We are his workmanship in Christ, created for good works.[5] Even our physical scars in motherhood are a shadow of God's costly grace.

CONSUMMATION: Our Body and Gospel Stewardship

In this life, we will all glorify God with our bodies in different ways, but regardless, we must remember the temporal nature of our physical appearance. Ultimately, the physical body we hope for is the one that is raised with Christ when he returns and we become like him.[6] We don't have to have the perfect body today. We know that this time is short and that we'll have a perfectly restored body for eternity.

God Isn't Shaming Your Postpartum Body

Just as I had to counsel myself with truth before posting a newly postpartum picture to my Instagram feed, it's important to remember this phrase: "God isn't ashamed of my postpartum body."

How do I know this? Well for one, he doesn't spend a lot of time addressing what our physical appearance is supposed to look like in Scripture. Instead he spends most of the Bible pressing into heart attitudes and motivations. While we are busy judging and sizing up who is a better mom based on her postpartum figure or a more put together woman based on external appearances, God

---

[5] Ephesians 2:10.

[6] Philippians 3:20-21.

looks on the heart. He is concerned with a different type of beauty. In fact, Jesus wasn't even physically attractive in a way that met his culture's expectations.[7]

God is concerned with things like laziness, gluttony, idolatry, selfishness, and pride. Are we careless with our bodies? Do we use them for our own purposes, or do we carefully consider how to make the best use of them for his purposes?

God is also concerned with our spirit. Is it peaceful, quiet, and trusting in him? Does it focus on the eternal and unseen, or do we spend a lot of time fretting about the temporary advantages of physical beauty? Are we trying to be "body positive" without acknowledging the origin of our worth, surrendering our bodies to Christ?

We can turn to God in worship today with a right desire for health that makes it about him, not us. Instead of shaming our postpartum selves for having a mommy tummy, or priding ourselves in our ability to craft a better-than-before-baby body, let's submit our whole lives to God. He might remind us of the wisdom in physical training, eating differently, or making time for strategic health decisions. Or he might prompt us to get some extra rest instead of hitting the gym again (which might not erase the rolls but allows you to be more pleasant when your kids are awake).

But let's remember that the great commission isn't about going out into the world and preaching, "Moms, you don't have to look like you've had a baby. You can take control of your life and erase the effects of childbearing!" Instead we are called to lay down our perceived rights, boasting in Christ alone, who has the power to save and bring lasting joy for those who are lost in the world.

Turn Your Gaze

After all that, it's normal to still feel confused about how God practically leads us in the struggle with postpartum body image. Because even in our best intentions, we're still limited.

---

[7] Isaiah 53:2.

We're limited by the far-reaching effects of the fall in our postpartum bodies and circumstances. Sleep deprivation, busy schedules, people with urgent needs, hormones, birthing injuries, limited financial resources, lack of help, and more prevent us from doing all we can to have bodies in peak physical condition. And even in this, we must trust that he can still receive glory in our weakness.

Our spirit can display a lovely contentment in situations where exercise, antiwrinkle cream, expensive under-eye concealer, and special diet programs just aren't reasonable options. We can display true beauty as people see us preoccupied with loving others in the name of Jesus instead of obsessing over our muffin top.

We're also bound by the realities of our human body. He didn't design us to survive on a steady diet of donuts, fried chicken, and milkshakes. We probably can't succumb to long-term physical idleness without consequences later in life. The endorphins released through exercise really can help us mentally and emotionally recover from the stress of child-rearing. Health is a good gift from God, and we should invest in it where we can.

In both cases, we sometimes attempt to live beyond our human limits because of pride.[8] The antidote to pride isn't trying harder to be perfect, but embracing the only one who is. Our limitations point us to our need for the Savior. Regardless of how God is shaping our hearts as we battle body image after baby, it's all about our worship of him and participation in his big story (not being the star of our own story).

Where are your eyes resting, Mama? On your ill-fitting sweatpants? On your friend's tighter tummy? On your Instagram feed? On that new top you think will finally cover your postpartum stomach? On your hope in your ability to make it to the gym every day this week?

Or are your eyes resting on God's faithfulness to you in Christ and your participation in the wonderful call to make disciples of those in your life, especially

---

[8] Hannah Anderson's book *Humble Roots* (Chicago, IL: Moody, 2016) does a thorough job of exploring humility in our limitations and greatly influenced my thinking.

your children? Turn your eyes upon Jesus. Your rolls might not go away, but your preoccupation with yourself just might.

DISCUSSION QUESTIONS

1. How have you struggled with postpartum body image? Is it a big part of your thought life or your actions? Why or why not?

2. What does God want you to focus on and devote your time to? How do God's values change how you view your body?

3. Taking your time, resources, and limitations into account, how will you steward your body as a gift from God?

10

THE GOSPEL
AND OUR FOOD CHOICES

Laura

Every morning it's the same. Oatmeal and peanut butter (with a few added raisins for a little fun), served in primary-colored bowls at the kitchen island. I've been a fan of this simple routine for a while now. It fills tummies until at least 10:00 a.m., and I don't have to deal with pint-sized preferences while I'm still waking up. (Three cheers for even the tiniest mom victories.)

But there was a time when this breakfast wasn't so simple.

My firstborn was just over a year old when I started introducing solids. The familiar red-capped jar of peanut butter sat in our pantry, and I assumed if it was good enough for my husband and me, it was good enough for our prized possession sitting in the high chair. But after seeing a question pop up on a Facebook group, an unsuspecting pantry staple (my faithful go-to) suddenly represented a dangerous decision that needed careful consideration if I were to be qualified as a caring, intentional mother.

The moms online were talking about the dangers of refined sugars, artificial sweeteners, coloring additives, and emulsifiers. Let's just say there were a lot of five-dollar words thrown around that I never associated with my beloved spread. Not only that, they were discussing the latest research on when and how to introduce peanut butter to a baby to avoid allergies: after the age of one, as early as possible, in the pediatrician's office, straight out of the jar, by adding hot water and making it into a puree, and only if you've blended organic peanuts in your own food processor at home. The opinions and quoted research tossed around the virtual room appeared faster than I could read them. I felt the familiar pang of mom guilt well up in my chest as I sank into the sticky world of peanut butter and children.

This feeling of guilt associated with food has been a familiar foe during my time as a mom. It appeared when I tried to hide the formula canister at a mom's group. After I ate goat cheese without thinking while pregnant. When I realized I served regular chocolate chip cookies to a friend's child who preferred to feed her children a gluten-free diet. The countless times I've served processed foods when my husband worked late into the night.

The voice whispers, "Have you served enough vegetables today? Was that snack too close to supper? Should you make a vinegar wash for those strawberries since they're not organic? It might be annoying, but the only peanut butter you should buy is the kind you have to stir." The options for inducing food-related guilt are endless, and the pressures on my soul surrounding food are straight from culture.

Culture's Message: Superfood, Superhuman

These days we are told you can use food to achieve almost anything. Want to lose the postpartum pooch? There's a diet for that. Stop your child from acting out? Here's what to stop feeding them. Struggling with post-baby hair regrowth? Add this powder to your morning smoothie. Need to get rid of your child's dry skin? Try rubbing this cooking oil on it a few times a day.

If you feed them the right foods, grown in the right way and cooked using the right methods, you're doing the right thing. Food is fuel. Food is a lifestyle. Food is acceptance. Food is the ultimate healer. Food is power and status.

Of course, sugar-free, gluten-free, vegetarian, and other diets can provide legitimate help. Sometimes we or our children must avoid certain foods because of mild or even life-threatening allergies or health needs—which should always be considered and attended to. But other times, we make a lot of unnecessary rules about food based on preferences and trendy diets or the latest viral articles.

The pressure starts the day a woman becomes a mother as she's faced with how she'll sustain her infant. It only gets more intense as her child grows and she introduces first foods (Egg whites? Smashed avocado? Iron-fortified oat cereal?) and deals with picky toddlers, crazy daily schedules, meals on the go, school lunches, Sunday potlucks, soccer snack schedules, and school regulations for birthday treats. Good mothers monitor breast and bottle, forks and spoons. They measure the extent of her love, the quality of her care, and the depth of her devotion to her child's well-being.

As her family grows and changes, the latest research on the best diets and foods to serve the people she loves the most changes along with it. Laboring to keep up with nutrition trends sometimes feels more exhausting than raising toddlers. Not to mention, it's deeply discouraging to any mothers who don't have the luxury of time or money to be particular about what they put on the table.

Food does matter, and it actually plays an iconic part of the gospel story (the fruit in the garden, anyone?), but God's message surrounding food and feeding our families is different from what the culture tells us. Caring about food is not bad, but God finds more value in what we feed the heart than what we feed the stomach. Food's ability to heal and nourish our bodies after the fall is limited. But Christ can fully heal both the body and the spirit for eternity.

The Gospel Message

CREATION: Edible Eden

The first food man and woman ate would have put any of our "100 percent organic" diets to shame. Planted by God, locally grown produce filled the Garden of Eden, all of it free of pesticides, chemicals, additives, fertilizers, and dyes. The farming in Eden would have been prolific, beautiful, and perfectly nutritious for sustaining life. Adam and Eve never went hungry, there was no such

EVE EATING
THE FRUIT
WAS ONLY AN
OUTWARD SIGN
OF HER
INNER DOUBT

thing as a peanut allergy, and unhealthy fats weren't something to worry about. It was a foodie's paradise.

God declared all the plants, the animals, and the entire earth "good" and his image-bearers "very good."[1] God gave Adam and Eve every seed, plant, fruit, and tree to them to eat in the garden—except the tree of the knowledge of good and evil.[2] Out of the endless buffet of herbs, fruits, and vegetables for them to enjoy, only one was off-limits.

But it was the one they couldn't resist.

FALL: The Forbidden Fruit

With one bite of a perfect, locally grown, chemical-free, farm-to-table fruit, our relationship with God was severed. But Eve eating the fruit was only an outward sign of her inner doubt and desire to taste something other than God. With a bite of the forbidden, suddenly the world of food and our relationship to it came crashing down.

Where before only one tree was banned, God's people were eventually given meticulous food laws. Prohibiting things like pork and shellfish, the complex set of food rules set them apart from other nations.[3] There were rules on what to eat, when to eat, how to eat, and how to prepare the meal.

On the day of original sin, God cursed the ground with thorns, thistles, and sweat on our brows.[4] The earth now groans under the curse. Farmers toil and labor to produce enough crops and livestock to feed the world's population, yet the harvest never reaches some of the neediest people. People wake up and go to bed hungry. Children cry out for food their mother can't provide. Entire countries suffer from malnutrition, and millions die from starvation every year. The food we have spoils and rots, pests and dangerous bacteria threaten it, and

---

[1] Genesis 1:31.

[2] Genesis 1:29; 2:16-17.

[3] Leviticus 11:1-47.

[4] Genesis 3:17-19.

it can negatively affect our bodies through things like allergies, addiction, heart disease, and diabetes.

We feel the curse in our homes too. The table is a battleground. We coerce our toddlers to "try at least three bites," we fight our own urge to overeat brownies while hiding in the pantry, and we play a ruthless game of tug-of-war with decisions about breastfeeding and bottle feeding. It's the struggle, the necessity, the bruised cycle of food.

The fall also severed our relationship with others. Now we hold back from hospitality or fellowship out of fear we won't be up on the latest diets or we'll inadvertently serve something that might cause someone else to have an allergic reaction. We avoid gathering around the table because it takes too much time, energy, and effort. We don't want to risk damaging our relationships—or our perfectly executed diets. We dance and stammer around the topic of food choices, sometimes holding our judgments close to our chest, other times at the ready to educate anyone who might nudge open the door of opportunity. We want to enlighten, inform, and convert others to our way of thinking. We find our validation, worth, and worship in food.

REDEMPTION: The Bread of Life

But God knew the tailspin that something as ordinary as dinner would send us into, and he sent his Son, Jesus, to stop the descent. We can't heal our broken bodies by feeding our children more vegetables than fruit snacks (though we are tempted to try). Only Christ's broken body on the cross can give us true redemption and freedom from our sin. When Jesus came and fulfilled the law, he removed the restrictions on food laws. As he walked on the dry, cracked, unforgiving soil of this earth, he gave clear instructions on our relationship with food, declaring all foods clean.[5]

Because of Christ's work, we don't find our identity in special food rules or diets. We still want to be wise stewards of our bodies, but we know we are not

---

[5] Mark 7:18-19.

set apart or made more godly by avoiding certain foods, nor should we feel ashamed or embarrassed by what's in our refrigerators.[6] The decision for breast-feeding or bottle feeding doesn't have to lead us to stressful Google searches because our trust isn't in a preferred method—it's in Jesus. Because of Christ, we are all welcome at the table. We find our righteousness in him alone rather than how we do our grocery shopping. We can be kind to those who make different decisions from ours, and we can forgive when someone forgets our needs or preferences. We boast in the cross rather than our cooking.[7]

CONSUMMATION: Farm-to-Table for Eternity

Someday, when we join our Savior in the eternal Eden, our battle with food will end. At that time, people and the rest of creation will be made perfect.[8] As we're united with Christ on the new earth, we'll no longer argue about food preferences and organic certifications or struggle with yo-yo dieting and stress eating. Allergies will be a thing of the past, and fearmongering memes won't keep us up at night worrying about the hot dogs we served for lunch.

We'll finally enjoy a bountiful, high-producing garden free of weeds or rocky soil. We will still work it, but it will be gloriously free of vain toil and labor.[9] Food will still be an essential part of our eternal lives, just as it is today. We'll join our Savior in the most amazing farm-to-table dinner party for eternity, full of well-aged wines and rich, delicious food.[10]

An Open Table

I live in Iowa, in the heart of the Midwest—also known as the breadbasket—and it's not uncommon to hear moms debating the merits of biotech and GMOs, organic certifications, food sourcing, and more. I wish I could tell you

---

[6] Romans 14:7-8.

[7] Galatians 6:14.

[8] Romans 8:20-23.

[9] Isaiah 65:21-23.

[10] Isaiah 25:6.

I've always been an innocent bystander in these conversations (especially when they've become heated), but honestly, I haven't. I've spouted off facts from the internet I read during a late-night nursing session. I've repeated what a friend who works in the ag industry said. I've silently judged another mom's opinion—sometimes she's "too strict and clean," and other times I want to hand her a bag of brussels sprouts.

More often than I'd like to admit, I've found myself aligned with the legalists we read about in the New Testament. Some of the believers in the early church were getting into heated debates about food rules and regulations. Some felt they needed to abstain from certain foods, and others felt the food rules didn't apply to them. In Romans 14, Paul addresses this topic head-on. He tells the church to stop quarreling over food. Because of Christ's defeat of death, all food is declared clean. There is freedom in food choice. How one eats is a matter of personal conscience.[11]

Paul reminds us we are not the standard and judge of another person. Because Jesus fulfilled the law, we don't find our value in restricting certain foods in our diets, nursing to the requisite one-year mark, or aligning with the latest food fad. God welcomes all believers—ones who live with strict diets and others who will eat anything in front of them—and we should too.[12] Bodily training, and the food that fuels it, is of some value, but let's not act like our salvation hangs in the balance over it.[13]

Preferences or Obsessions?

I have several friends who prefer organic meats and produce. I have other friends who shop the sales and look for rock-bottom prices. Still others opt to purchase their meat, eggs, and in-season produce from a local farmer. I even

---

[11] Romans 14:1-4.

[12] Romans 14:3-4.

[13] 1 Timothy 4:8.

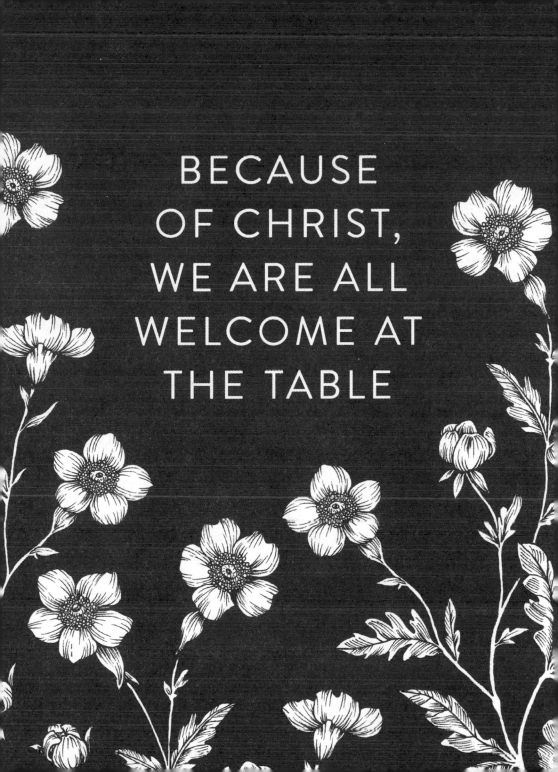

have friends who raise some of their own meat and grow many of their own fruits and vegetables.

Carefully and thoughtfully feeding your family is not wrong. In fact, it's loving and merciful to protect someone from an allergy, curate a well-balanced meal plan, and ensure everyone has the proper provision of vitamins and nutrients to have energy for their day. Not only that, but God made food for our enjoyment as we serve him. It's for celebration! We can (and should) delight in the sound of a sizzling pan, the sight of the deep green of a cucumber, and the smell of a perfectly seared steak.

The problem lies when we judge, condemn, and criticize others for not holding the same view we do. It becomes sin when it clouds our vision so much we can't love those around us simply because they eat differently from us. In fact, it's easy for me to forget that while I can zip off to my local grocery store to pick up anything I have an appetite for, some mothers would be grateful to simply serve a dinner that fills their babies' empty bellies. Food choice is a good gift from a gracious God, and not everyone gets to experience redemption in this way.

Do you feel frustration with a mom on a playdate for serving cookies as a snack 15 minutes before you sit down for lunch? Do you eye roll at the mom who wants to keep her baby sugar-free until age one? Are you haunted over the piece of cheesecake you ate at a friend's birthday party?

Our response when a fellow mom breaks our food barriers, particularly with our children, is telling of the state of our hearts. If we're restless, constantly checking our children's diets, stressing over where we're going to buy our groceries, or secretly hoping to convert friends to our way of living, we've taken our food preferences too far. The question is, Is your identity found in a diet or fad you want you or your family to follow? Or is it resting in Christ despite what is served on a playdate?

Let's take the posture of a humble, grateful heart, receiving our food with thanksgiving as a provision from our Father, and recognize God released us from his judgment—and from judging others.[14] Because of the gospel of Jesus Christ, we can shop, cook, and feed our families in freedom.

DISCUSSION QUESTIONS

1. In what ways do you view food as a measuring stick of your ability to be a good mother?

2. How does your identity in Christ remove the need for food-related worry, leading you instead to worship God for his provision and goodness in your life? Is there a specific area of misplaced worship you need to repent of?

3. How does the freedom of the gospel empower you to extend grace to others with different food preferences, and who can you do that for today?

---

[14] 1 Timothy 4:3-5.

11

THE GOSPEL
AND OUR RELATIONSHIPS

Emily

When our first child was just over six months old, my husband and I prepared to spend our first night away. Naturally, I wrote the grandparents a handbook.

Here's a small quote from the section on sleeping (yes, the handbook had so many topics, it needed sections):

> He goes to bed between 7:00 and 8:00 p.m. Watch for tired signals!
> Putting him to bed closer to 7:00 or 7:30 p.m. is best. If you're going
> to give him a bath, start it after 6:30 so it can lead into the bedtime
> routine. Here's the rest of the routine: Go into a dimly lit room, give
> him a clean diaper, put on pajamas, put on the sleep sack, give him
> a bottle, give him a pacifier, and rock him to sleep. Lay him down
> on his back when he is drowsy but still awake with no blankets or
> animals in his crib. If his white noise is on and the room is dark, he
> will generally go straight to bed or will do so with minimal crying.

It's okay to laugh at me. I'm laughing at me (and most likely, so were Grandma and Grandpa). My intentions for this handbook seemed good. I wanted my son to have the comforts of Mommy and Daddy in the arms of other quality caregivers. But underneath that layer of good intentions, my harmful heart attitudes demanded...

"Grandma and Grandpa need to meet my expectations in order to love my son and make me happy."

"I am the only person who knows how to care for my child. Anyone else will do an insufficient job of meeting his needs."

"Anyone who respects me will adhere to all of my ways and preferences."

Those phrases didn't make it into the handbook, but my expectations, preferences, and standards were a recipe for relational strain.

Both sets of grandparents showed patience as we worked out the kinks in this new aspect of our relationship, but the process wasn't without bumps. As you'd imagine, they couldn't always follow our rules. We didn't always have fair expectations. We couldn't communicate or understand one another perfectly every time.

Years later, I'm doing good if I provide instructions as I hand off all the big and little ones to grandparents, hollering "Thanks—see ya later!" as I'm walking out the door. We still communicate the essentials, but I'm getting better at trusting God, trusting others (who are worthy of trust), and recognizing I don't own a patent on the one right way of caregiving.

Culture's Message: Mom's Way or the Highway

Relationships in motherhood are complicated. There's tension with the grandparents for not following your snack schedule, awkwardness with your friend at church who thinks kids should always be in service when you're fine utilizing the nursery, uncomfortable conversations with the mom who thinks breastfeeding can always work if you just try hard enough, wrong reactions when you've just had a miscarriage and your friend complains about her pregnancy, and so on.

Each relationship, conversation, and interaction has the potential to threaten your identity in motherhood, making you feel ashamed or small. Or you can choose to rise above, not caring what other people think because your way is the only way that matters. All these issues lead to things like brokenness, isolation, and unforgiveness in our relationships.

Western culture is highly individual, elevating the self and personal choice above the good of others or the feelings of the group. When personal choice is worshipped, we believe all other people should tolerate, encourage, and further our individual preferences. In recent decades, this has also become the framework for motherhood and the lens through which we view our relationships with others.

When others don't adhere to our expectations or the unwritten handbook we've crafted for our children, we respond by outwardly or passively withholding love, fellowship, and the joy of our children. Culture tells us that to have peace in relationships, we must agree with and affirm another's preferences. Kindness is given only when kindness is shown. If someone wants to respect us, they'll affirm all that we do and encourage our freedom to do whatever seems right to us.

Even within the family unit, Mom often has the upper hand in childcare decisions, lifestyle preferences, and methods of nurturing. So sometimes, it really comes down to the adage, "It's mom's way or the highway." Culture can make it seem like Dad's opinion (especially during the little years) is silly, uninformed, and inferior to Mama Bear's well-honed instincts.

Is this God's plan for our relationships? To love, accept, and enjoy only those who meet our social expectations and affirm (or at least tolerate) our preferred way of life?

Despite the complexity of our relationships in motherhood, Christ's provision and example for us in the gospel helps us extend grace, enact justice, and overlook offenses in conflicts big and small.

A Quick Caveat

Relationships have different levels of health. This chapter is mainly addressing the offenses, heartaches, and tensions that arise from misplaced expectations, different choices, mildly bad influences, and moments of relational ugliness—the "normal" conflicts and stressors we experience in our everyday lives. However, relationships where there is abuse (physical, emotional, or sexual) or otherwise extremely unhealthy influence or behavior happening (substance abuse, strong profanity, racism, ongoing mental health concerns, and so on) will likely need to be dealt with in a different way than presented in this chapter. God always calls followers of Christ to forgiveness, but he also calls us to protection and justice. It's right to set boundaries in relationships out of love, contacting the appropriate authorities when needed. Discerning those situations is best done in community with other believers who can help you know how to best protect your heart and mind and the hearts and minds of your children.

The Gospel Message

CREATION: God's Way or the Highway

When God created Adam and Eve, he gave them instructions (a handbook of sorts) for life on Earth. God's expectations for his new people were rooted in love, essential for their thriving and for their very life. He wanted a relationship with them, but a relationship with a holy God required complete obedience to his clearly communicated commands.

He provided the creation mandate: "Be fruitful and multiply and fill the earth and subdue it, and have dominion over the fish of the sea and over the birds of the heavens and over every living thing that moves on the earth" (Genesis 1:28). Adam and Eve were to use "every plant yielding seed that is on the face of all the earth, and every tree with seed in its fruit" for food (Genesis 1:29), but they weren't allowed to eat from the tree of the knowledge of good and evil.[1]

While the first people were given responsibility and authority (as we are as parents), they weren't the gods of the garden. Instead they carried out their perfect parent's plan for life in his creation.

---

[1] Genesis 2:16-17.

FALL: Taking Our Own Road

But instead of going God's way, obeying his commands in the garden, Adam and Eve disobeyed with doubting hearts, eating from the forbidden tree after being tempted by a serpent.[2] They did what seemed best to them, elevating personal desires over God's corporate creation mandate. As Adam and Eve rejected God's ways, we all inherited sin.[3]

We follow in their footsteps, rejecting the truth of God's good design in exchange for our view of the world.[4] Particularly as moms, this means we craft our own handbook for our children with voiced and unvoiced expectations in our relationships. If our children aren't allowed to use an iPad or eat brownies before dinner, and we see others breaking our laws, we sound the trumpets and bring in the army.

Or maybe it's subtler. We think, "It's okay for your child, but don't tell me how to parent mine. I'm the god of this garden, and I decide what's best." When someone questions our lifestyle, challenges our choices, or gives us their contrary opinion, we brood and complain, waiting for a moment to show displeasure in a passive way. We strategically withhold fellowship from people who disobey our parenting rules or make us feel like less than amazing moms because compromising feels like failing in the job at which we most want to succeed.

It's not that we shouldn't have ideals or standards in parenthood. It's good to have plans and desires for our children. The problem comes when we think our preferences are the highest good for ourselves and our children, seeing others' comments and choices as an offense against us instead of looking to God's Word as our standard in life and relationships.

REDEMPTION: Christ Makes a New Way

Instead of rejecting us forever for rebelling against his ways, God provided

---

[2] Genesis 3:6.

[3] Genesis 3:5.

[4] Romans 1:25.

a way for reconciliation. He knew we couldn't obey his good, perfect, and holy commands. The only path to freedom came through an act of divine justice.[5]

God sent his Son—who never gave in to the temptation to make his own way—to be sin for us so that we might know and follow God's path for our lives through Christ.[6] Jesus purchased our ability to have a right relationship with God, free from the expectation of fulfilling all his laws, by taking the punishment we deserve: God's wrath, his absence of fellowship, his strong arm of justice, and his right to get even.[7]

Our response to this should prevent us from being like the unforgiving servant in Matthew 18:21-35 and like the condemned Pharisees in Matthew 23:4-7. God's radical reconciliation and grace toward us through Christ when we've failed to meet his good and perfect expectations means we should extend radical grace to others, forgiving them, "seventy-seven times."[8] It also means we need to humble ourselves before our Messiah, valuing relationship and servanthood over our burdensome personal preferences.

CONSUMMATION: The Path to a Better Eden

One day, when every knee bows before him, our handbooks for motherhood will be embarrassingly insignificant compared to the revelation of his perfect plan. He will avenge, repay, and judge every wrong committed.[9] We don't have to dole out revenge or withhold love on Earth, because we know resolution is coming when Christ returns and Satan is thrown into the lake of fire.[10] We can look forward to the time when we'll share in perfect relationship with the family

---

[5] Romans 7:5-6.

[6] 2 Corinthians 5:21.

[7] Matthew 5:17.

[8] Matthew 18:21-22. "Seventy-seven times" is Jesus' way of saying Peter should forgive endlessly without keeping track.

[9] Hebrews 10:30.

[10] Revelation 20:10.

of God—embodied, resurrected persons who love, enjoy, and celebrate God's way forever, even with our many different preferences.

Grace Isn't a Free Pass

We can start to wrap our minds around this costly reconciliation that God gives us in Christ, but it doesn't always translate into daily life. When Grandma and Grandpa put the baby to bed two hours later than we requested or we hear they watched a movie we'd consider too scary, the question remains, How do we offer grace without giving others a free pass to do whatever they want?

Although I don't know the answer to that question for every situation, more and more I find myself asking, "Is this a *personal preference* I'm holding on to with an unloving grip, or is this a *harmful sin* against God and my child that needs to be confronted in love?" More often than not, in the context of relationships with trustworthy people, it's an uncomfortable violation of my mommy handbook that I can cover with a gracious attitude.[11]

Is This a Personal Preference?

Did someone forget to have the correct snack for your child's preferred diet at the birthday party?[12] Consider believing the best of their intentions and offering them a genuine thank-you for the great celebration. What an excellent teaching opportunity for your child as you remind them that things won't always be easy or comfortable. People won't always think about our preferences, but we can still love them. We can take heart and remember a verse like Proverbs 19:11: "Good sense makes one slow to anger, and it is his glory to overlook an offense."

Is This a Harmful Sin That Needs to Be Confronted?

Sometimes it's hard to differentiate our personal preferences from harmful

---

[11] 1 Peter 4:8.

[12] This example is *not* referring to someone with a severe or life-threatening food allergy, which probably needs to be handled and confronted in a serious, direct way.

sins. Either way, we can move forward from a posture of humility. From a heart of forgiveness, which is more concerned about loving God's good design than having people adhere to our design, we can address sin and pursue reconciliation where it's needed. A mom who's gotten the log out of her own eye (seeing her own errors, her own sins, her own need for grace) can more effectively address the speck (sin issue) in another's eye.[13]

If your friend failed to correct her aggressive child after several playdates, the process of forgiveness and reconciliation might include a frank but gentle conversation about what hurt you or your child. If you and your husband are about to embark on a trip with your in-laws, the process might include a preventative discussion about relational boundaries. Christian love brings sin before the true Judge, looking for ways for relationships to exist with minimal harm from sin's effects.

Reflections on Gospel-Rooted Relationships

We sat around the table at the fanciest restaurant in our little town for a post-bedtime night out, each woman ordering something different. The drinks arrived first: herbal tea, cups of chai, decaf coffee with cream, and bottled water. Next came the food and desserts: roasted cauliflower, crusty bread, crème brûlée, flourless chocolate cake, and blueberry galette. Each woman's dish and drink were different, but each ordered from the same menu.

When I looked around, I observed that the lives of the women present were as varied as the food and drinks in front of us. We included women whose ages spanned various decades, women who worked outside of the home, women who volunteered, women who stayed at home full-time. Some held master's degrees, some owned small businesses, some were taking seminary classes, and others were trying to decide what to do in life's next season. Among this group, mission fields ranged from the home front to the ends of the earth. Some women were reaching small neighborhoods in rural areas, some were ministering to at-risk

---

[13] Matthew 7:1-5.

moms at a local women's clinic, some were loving babies through foster care, and others were getting to know Muslims with the hope of sharing the gospel.

Public school moms. Private school moms. Homeschool moms. Moms who breastfed, moms who pumped, moms who gave their babies formula. Moms who experienced the pains of longing for children, pregnancy scares, or children with special needs. Moms of two kids and moms of five kids. Moms who have help with childcare and moms who shoulder the brunt of child-rearing. Moms with six-figure household incomes and moms who rejoice and make do on a small ministry income.

Moms—all ministering differently, all dying to self in various ways, all following and loving their Lord Jesus, and all living out the gospel in ways unique to their family, passions, and circumstances. In him and through him and because of him, we enjoyed both lighthearted and deep conversation with fellowship and joy.

And although this moment around a dinner table was idyllic, it was a small reflection of the relationships we can have when our hopes, expectations, and identities are rooted in Christ.

We don't have to elevate our handbook for motherhood as the best way when we can acknowledge God's way as the only way—a road we can all walk only with humility through the person and work of Christ. We're not in competition; we're in community. When we seek the greater good of the kingdom over our own personal preferences and desires—when we prioritize reconciliation and understanding—relationships can thrive amid imperfection and even offenses.

DISCUSSION QUESTIONS

1. What relationships (friends, grandparents, coworkers…) have been most challenging to you in motherhood and why? How much are the challenges due to your personal preferences as opposed to specific, ongoing sin?

2. In what ways have you failed to live up to God's standards? How has he dealt with this in Christ? How should that change the way you relate in your challenging relationships?

3. Consider an upcoming situation where you might experience relational strain. How could you proactively pray, plan, and speak truth so you're ready to handle it with grace, truth, and love?

THE GOSPEL
AND OUR TRADITIONS

Laura

I stepped back and admired my work. Twenty-five brown paper bags hung from a tree branch with yarn and clothespins. I thought it needed more Christmas spirit, so I added a few pine branches from my backyard and a stem of faux red berries. "There. Now, that's a perfect Advent calendar," I thought.

Day one. I am filled wonder and delight. Yes, my two- and three-year-old kids ripped the bag and ran around during the Bible story, but we were doing it! A completed snowman sticker activity was hung on the wall. I spoke the story of Adam and Eve in the same room as them, and they seemed breathless with anticipation for the fulfillment of the promise. (Or maybe just for a candy cane, but who can know for sure?) I was the best mom in the land.

Day five. I'm frustrated. We tried to drive around to see Christmas lights, but apparently everyone's heart in our neighborhood was two sizes too small. We saw a few lights but nothing impressive. My three-year-old repeated "Where are dey? Where are dey?" a million times. Our youngest melted down in the car because we had her up too late. Hot chocolate spilled and needed to be cleaned out of the car seat. We skipped the Bible story and swiftly got everyone to bed.

Day ten. I am jaded. Go ahead, kids—destroy the homemade sugar cookies

I spent all day laboring over. Snowflake-shaped cookies are ugly anyway. What's the point if you're just going to beg me to eat 15 of them, spill sprinkles all over the floor, and need to be hosed down before bed because of all the frosting in your hair? Why do I even try with this "building memories" stuff?

Day 17. I am hopeless. Daddy worked late and missed the activity time—again. All the kids want to know is when they get to "*ooopen presents!*" I don't have the energy to complete the night's activity, so I give them a piece of chocolate, to which they reply, "More, more, more!" Verbally and in sign language. Awesome.

Four weeks later, the Advent calendar is skewed haphazardly toward the ceiling, three bags are ripped, one is missing, and there are more pine needles on my couch than on the branch. The calendar's wonky state is a picture of my heart. Where did this all go wrong? Traditions and memories are supposed to be special and magical, and all I felt was defeat and discouragement. How do other moms do it?

Culture's Message: Perfect Pomp and Pageantry

Of course, my overzealous efforts to create meaningful traditions have not been confined to Advent. Easter, Thanksgiving, birthdays, family quiet times, or mealtime prayers—it doesn't matter if it's a daily ritual or a once-a-year event—I've always had a knack for making traditions a bigger deal than they are, losing my focus on what's most important.

I don't think I'm alone in this.

Secular culture and the church alike place a high value on traditions—making them exciting, fun, and full of pomp, wonder, and delight! Television and movies showcase magical, elaborately decorated homes for Christmas, huge birthday parties with bounce houses and circus performers, and Thanksgiving feasts straight out of a Norman Rockwell painting.

Social media hasn't helped, displaying scenes that were once reserved for Hollywood and giving the impression that every family home celebrates in the same extravagant way. Moments frozen in time look picture-perfect. The children are attentive, the cinnamon rolls bakery-worthy, the Easter baskets adorable, the activities thoughtful and well executed, and the birthday party decor straight out of a magazine. Everything is gorgeous and spectacular, and everyone is happy and getting along. The pictures are pinned, the blog posts are saved, and the standard is set for mom to love her family well in traditions through decor, planning, and activities.

On top of that, in Christian circles, we put extra pressure on making sure there's deeper meaning in the tradition, which must be flawlessly taught by knowledgeable parents and well received by eager children. A mom must stay up to date on the latest Christian children's books and music, special vocabulary cards, Scripture memory systems, Advent calendars, and Holy Week coloring pages. We can feel as if missing a day of intentional teaching and educating means our precious time is lost and our children may never know the ways of the Lord. Moms chat online and in person about a new product they've purchased or a new system they've set in place to "plant solid biblical truths deep in their child's heart." The pressures build, one after the other, until a mom can no longer bear it.

When plans go awry—when the kids want to talk about presents more than Jesus, when the day just feels too full and the family quiet time is missed—a mom can feel devastated. Her motherhood has fallen short, and she needs to figure out how to improve to be a "good mom." On other days, when her plans somehow magically come together, she is elated—for a moment. Then, her heart begins the wrestling match with pride and meeting the standard again.

Before she knows it, she is bound and tied by the success or failure of family traditions.

Traditions are good things—biblical even. But God does not promise they'll always go smoothly, especially with children involved, nor does he ask for a perfect execution that blows away the other neighborhood moms. Instead he looks at the heart. God didn't design traditions to impress others; he designed them to remember and to celebrate his work.

So the question is, When all the pageantry is stripped away—the balloons popped, the wreaths stored, the coloring sheets used up, and the party plates thrown in the trash—what do you have left?

The Gospel Message

CREATION: Significant Routines

A tradition is usually thought of as something you do with regularity, but it's more than working out each morning or having a piece of dark chocolate after dinner each night. We usually refer to those as habits or routines. The word "tradition" means "the handing down of information, beliefs, and customs by word of mouth or by example from one generation to another without written instruction."[1] It's something we do with regularity but with added meaning. And biblically, we find a tradition is anything done routinely but with the added significance of remembering God, celebrating his work, and teaching his ways to those around us.

The word "tradition" isn't found in the Old Testament, but if we look carefully, we find traditions starting all the way back in the creation account. When God finished his work of creating the heavens and the earth, plant and animal, man and woman, he rested from his work, blessing the seventh day and making it holy. In the Ten Commandments, God tells his people, "Remember the Sabbath day, to keep it holy…For in six days the LORD made heaven and earth, the sea, and all that is in them, and rested on the seventh day."[2] God set a tradition in place, making a regular way for his people to honor and remember what he had done.

FALL: Significant Selves

But like our first parents, our natural bent is to remember and celebrate ourselves rather than God. Like us, the Israelites had annual traditions, such as the Passover (to remember how God rescued them out of slavery in Egypt), the Feasts of Booths (to remember their journey in the wilderness from Egypt to Canaan), and the Feast of Unleavened Bread (to remember their haste in leaving Egypt). They also had more frequent traditions, like the Sabbath, daily sacrifices and offerings, and lessons for their children about God. "You shall teach

---

[1] *Merriam-Webster*, s.v. "tradition," www.merriam-webster.com/dictionary/tradition.

[2] Exodus 20:8,11.

them to your children, talking of them when you are sitting in your house, and when you are walking by the way, and when you lie down, and when you rise."[3] (It sounds a little like family discipleship might fit under this umbrella, right?)

As we progress through the Old Testament, we see the Israelites tended to go through the motions of traditions, giving lip service to God on the outside but remaining proud on the inside as they strove to look good, impress those around them, and earn God's favor. "This people honors me with their lips, but their heart is far from me; in vain do they worship me, teaching as doctrines the commandments of men."[4] Their traditions often celebrated their efforts and accomplishments rather than God's.

People haven't changed. As moms, we often spend more time mulling over the nutritional value and frosting color of our baby's smash cake than thanking God for our child's life, celebrating the Lord's good gifts over the past year, and looking ahead to what he will yet do. We hunt for the perfect Advent calendar mostly because we want to snap an adorable Instagram picture and less because we want our family to think about God's plan for redemption and the birth of our Savior.

Instead of using traditions to point to Christ, we use them to point to self.

REDEMPTION: Significant Sacrifice

But God knew we would twist tradition away from its true purpose and make it serve our own. We can easily change our outward behavior and go through the right motions, but changing our hearts is much more difficult. In fact, it's impossible to do on our own, which is why God sent and sacrificed his only Son. He knew we would never have real love for him on our own, so he made a way, meeting his impossible standard on our behalf. It is because of his great love for us that we can truly love at all. "We love because he first loved us."[5]

Now with the Holy Spirit at work within us, we can display our genuine love

---

[3] Deuteronomy 11:19.

[4] Mark 7:6-7.

[5] 1 John 4:19.

for God through the things we do rather than going through the motions but leaving our hearts behind. We can love our families through daily and annual traditions, understanding their true purpose is not about what we'll get but about remembering and honoring the one who gave us everything. Through traditions we can serve, knowing our status is secure in Christ, rather than worry about what others think of us or if we're doing enough. We can humbly teach what we know rather than act like know-it-alls. We can trust that salvation comes from God, not from our teaching through traditions. We can create memories with our families and friends to remember God rather than memorialize our own actions.

CONSUMMATION: Significant Savior

When Christ returns, it won't be hard to remember or honor God, because his dwelling place will be with us.[6] We won't be tempted by our own self-glory because his awe-inspiring glory will fill the earth and satisfy our roaming, hungry hearts. On that day, our history, memory, heirloom, heritage, and inheritance will walk among us. As daughters of God, we'll no longer need reminders throughout our day or year to call our wayward hearts back to the cross. Instead, every day we'll worship at the throne of our Lord and Savior.

Outward Appearance, Inward Attitude

"Okay, what did we read about yesterday? Does anyone remember?" I ask my family as we gather to talk about the Bible.

My question is met with a shake of the baby's rattle. My other two children are basically ignoring me—one is picking at the lint in the rug; another is making silly faces at Daddy, trying to get him to laugh.

I sigh. "Remember the twins? The hairy brother? The soup?"

"Can we have a snack?"

"Does this Bible have more pictures?"

"I like unicorns!"

"Is my birthday coming soon?"

---

[6] Revelation 21:3.

GOD CARES ABOUT
YOUR HEART'S AUTHENTIC,
WORSHIPFUL ACTION—NOT
EMPTY ACTIVITIES DONE
FOR THE SAKE OF SHOW

I decide to skip the review and jump into the next reading. Most of the night goes like this, me asking questions to distracted kids and my husband wrangling them on the rug and trying to help them engage. It feels a bit pointless. "Are they even listening? Will they ever remember this? Why do I feel so bad at this? I stink at teaching the Bible…" These thoughts run through my mind more days than I'd like to admit. Our tradition of trying to read and discuss the Bible each night before bed feels more like a duty than a delight.

That's because I've put my worth in wanting to see immediate fruit from our traditions. I want to hear my children regurgitate the story of Jacob and Esau perfectly so I can feel like a good mom. In those moments, I don't really care about God's glory on display. I just care about my glory and ego being soothed and comforted by feeling like I can check the box on teaching God's Word and creating special family memories—because sometimes, making my actions fall in line feels easier than dealing with my heart.

"You will not delight in sacrifice, or I would give it; you will not be pleased with a burnt offering. The sacrifices of God are a broken spirit; a broken and contrite heart, O God, you will not despise."[7] David knew performing all the outward traditions in the world couldn't save him from sin or give him a meaningful life. God is not looking for robots who do what they're told because the culture or the church says they should. God is always looking deeper. He "knows the secrets of the heart," and he "sees not as man sees: man looks on the outward appearance, but the LORD looks on the heart."[8]

This means God is much more concerned about your heart than about how well your resurrection rolls rise, whether you misspeak while telling the Christmas story (because, let's be real, it's hard to answer a four-year-old's questions about babies and virgins), whether your kid strips off their clothes during family worship time, or whether all your mom-friends are impressed by the latest curriculum you picked up. God cares about your heart's authentic, worshipful actions—not empty activities done for the sake of show.

[7] Psalm 51:16-17.

[8] Psalm 44:21; 1 Samuel 16:7.

A Tradition of Treasure and Testimony

When Christ is our greatest treasure, our love for him will spill over into our daily and special traditions. While it is a fine thing to think through how to teach catechisms or which Christmas traditions will serve our family best, God is only asking us to simply teach our children what he is teaching us. As God's Word deepens and grows in our own lives, he calls us to be faithful in sharing what we're learning to those around us.

Traditions are designed to reset our hearts, not to prove our worth. So let's stop overcomplicating things or setting the standard too high. Let's buck the cultural trend and lay aside our desire for perfection in traditions and short-term tangible success. Instead let's freely share the testimony of God in us. As moms who often set the tone of many of the traditions in our homes, let's trust in the slow build of a faithful, humble heart that is simply living out the love we have been shown. The cake can burn, the kids can act like crazy people, and the book can tear, yet we can rejoice and respond graciously as we model the gospel to those around us even when our traditions don't go as planned. Because all those activities don't make us right before God—Christ already has.

DISCUSSION QUESTIONS

1. How much pressure do you feel when celebrating family traditions? Do those celebrations sometimes define your status as a good mom? If so, how?

2. How does knowing your standing is secure in Christ change the way you view your family's traditions and how you feel when they don't go according to plan?

3. Do your family's traditions point to God as your greatest treasure and testimony? What adjustments might you make to display him more fully?

13

THE GOSPEL AND OUR CHRISTIAN COMMUNITY

Emily

"Your son may need a wheelchair."

He was just over two. Talking with a team of early intervention specialists about adaptations for the upcoming school year had wrung my heart dry. Tears flowed as I saw our new baby girl rolling, kicking, cooing, and blowing raspberries while her older brother sat and barely babbled along. But he shouldn't have been babbling. He should have been saying, "Mama, look—sister roll!" It was a hard week, to say the least.

I was exhausted, but my calendar reminded me that I'd signed up for a short weekend conference. If I went, I knew I'd have to shower, put on a smile, and talk to strangers (which was pretty much the last thing I felt like doing as I processed my son's limitations and eyed a week-old laundry mountain). But I went anyway. I took a dark, bumpy back road and suppressed tears as I swerved into the parking lot.

Then the situation took an unexpected turn.

As I entered the large auditorium, my pastor's wife greeted me and led me down the stairs to sit with a group from our church.

None of them knew it at the time, but I was blown away by God's comfort when I saw some of my closest mentors and dearest church family members sitting there. Instead of having me sit on the end of a row (I was there alone), one of the older couples sandwiched me between them. In the nearby rows, I saw my pastors, elders, and several older women from my church on every side. My heart rested. Although I was in a large group, I was not alone. Not at the conference, and much more important, not in all that I was facing at home.

When the worship session ended and we had a chance to talk, I shared what was on my heart. Not just the easy things but also the stuff about the wheelchair. They cried with me. Like a loving father, the man beside me put his arm around me, giving me a hug.

Although every part of me wanted to hide at home where I could wallow in fear, seeing people from my own church was exactly the encouragement and comfort I needed. Motherhood is hard sometimes, but we don't have to make it worse by being lone rangers or hiding from God's plan for our closest community.

Culture's Message: Like-Minded Moms Are Enough

We can't do motherhood alone. One solution to that problem? Find a community of peers—like-minded women who understand the situations you're dealing with. Over a cup of reheated coffee, you can share battle stories, laughing, commiserating, and helping one another get a grip.

When you struggle to breastfeed, fellow breastfeeding mamas can troubleshoot latch problems and tell you what helped them persevere. When you're overwhelmed by loud voices and wrestling bear cubs, moms of boys can laugh with you, providing tips for draining your kids' energy. When you shut yourself in the bathroom to get away from your exhausting toddler, fellow moms of littles can offer to bring you some wine and tell you, "I've been there too!" These groups help us feel safe, secure, and protected.

Peer communities aren't bad. Like-minded mom-friends in similar seasons with similar parenting philosophies can be immensely helpful and have a place—but culture tempts us to *stop there*. Funny mom movies, online groups, and community meet-ups make us feel as if peers are our only hope for help and friendship. But if they are our only hope, what happens if you can't find a peer-mom in the same situation as you? When you feel alone even though you're in a room full of women who "mom" just like you? When you're left wanting, knowing all the practical tips in the world won't help the deeper wounds in your heart? It begs the question, Are we too quickly satisfied with pats on the back, practical suggestions, and self-affirming personal relationships?

Peer groups can form deep communities, and the best of them can even point you to the gospel. But is this the only type of community God has designed for us? God desires for us to enjoy the common grace of relationships with those who have shared experiences, but have we pondered his eternal plan for community? Will all of God's saints look alike? Sound alike? Have the same experiences? Maybe God has more provision for us than our like-minded mom communities offer (even if they are offering us good truth). Through a body of believers in the local church, we can experience support for the soul, shaping through the Word, and opportunities to love others as we have been loved—even when ages span decades, experiences seem unrelated, and communication feels hard.

The Gospel Message

CREATION: A Good Plan for Community

The pull of our hearts toward others, especially those who have a united mission and shared values, is original to God's good design. God is one God in three persons—the Father, the Son, and the Holy Spirit. Although they are distinct in role and function, they are all equally God with a unified goal to bring God glory. Out of the overflow of the communal and loving relationship in the Trinity, God created people as image-bearers, first Adam and then Eve.[1] Why not just have one human? God said it wasn't good for man to be alone.[2]

Adam and Eve would labor together, carrying out the creation mandate in

---

[1] Genesis 1:26-27.

[2] Genesis 2:18.

complementary ways for God's glory as one flesh.[3] Sharing community and being on mission with different but like-hearted people, united in an unchangeable Person, was God's plan all along.

FALL: Community for Our Own Ends

Good fellowship grounded in God's commands didn't last long before sin entered the relationship. When Eve gave in to Satan's schemes, she encouraged her husband to join her in disobedience.[4] Then as fellow sinners, they hid together in shame. Instead of going to the Lord in immediate repentance, they succumbed to fear and avoided God.[5] When that didn't work, they turned against each other and played the blame game. This is the first picture of what happens when a community turns inward, unifying around their own interests. It leads to the deepest brokenness—and ultimately to death.

Because of Adam and Eve's sin, all human community is similarly stained. Instead of seeing ourselves as worshippers united with other believers in Christ to carry out God's mission, we are needy self-worshippers with a desire to have others adopt our plans and mission for life. Instead of congregating around love of God's Word and obedience to his commandments, we love our own standards and hold each other to them. Instead of seeking the genuine good of others, we find reason to gossip, grovel, complain, stir dissention, and band together over ungodliness if we think it will meet our felt needs.

Now when the struggles of motherhood come, we love answers that fit into our paradigm for life. We look for encouragement from people who don't expose the deeper issues in our hearts.

Satan especially hates God's community in the church, so he does whatever he can to hide its beauty. He makes sure we see the blemishes and recoil quickly to our supposedly safer peer communities. He makes us question what we might have to gain from an older woman who experienced motherhood two

---

[3] Genesis 2:24.

[4] Genesis 3:6-7.

[5] Genesis 3:8.

decades ago or what wisdom we might glean from a single woman in her forties. He makes sure our gospel communities are tough to break into, even though God knows they can strengthen us in the fierce battle against sin.

REDEMPTION: Community Established in the Church

Thankfully, God loved us too much to leave us with forever broken communities, where we look outside of his plan for us to find answers to our concerns. When we place our hope in Christ's death and resurrection, we all receive the Holy Spirit and are all adopted into God's family as heirs.[6] As brothers and sisters in Christ, we're part of what God is doing in the global church, but we're also called to take part in smaller groups of believers who have a unified mission within local communities.

God provides local churches where we can share in an unchanging, undefiled inheritance as part of one family.[7] Whether in an underground house church or a congregation of thousands in the Bible Belt, we get to serve together and love each other, manifesting God's glory until Jesus returns.[8]

In the Gospels, Jesus tells Peter (the rock) something amazing that should cause us to pause in wonder: "On this rock I will build my church, and the gates of hell shall not prevail against it" (Matthew 16:18). Jesus doesn't say that our breastfeeding support groups, boy mom tribes, or Facebook communities will prevail against hell—it will be his church. Jesus loved this community so much, he won her with his own blood.[9] Doesn't that make you want to be there and band together in God's bigger mission?

The church is where we encourage each other while we wait for Jesus to return. It's the family tasked with praying for us and helping us live like Jesus.[10] Even when we don't feel it or experience it on the first try, the truth is that Jesus

[6] Ephesians 1:5,13.

[7] 1 Peter 1:4.

[8] Ephesians 3:10.

[9] Acts 20:28.

[10] Ephesians 2:20-22; Colossians 3:16.

loves his bride, the church, so much that he's coming back for her. We should love her too.

CONSUMMATION: Christ's Bride in Community Forever

Like-minded mom communities sometimes encourage you to just hang on until the next group text, playdate, resource, or helpful post, but the Bible speaks of a living hope that never diminishes or returns void. That hope is in the resurrection and return of Christ.

Someday we'll worship with Christ's true bride, the church. The life experiences of these believers will span millennia, their stories and interests more colorful than your Instagram feed and held together in the person and work of Jesus. This is the type of community we should invest in now because it's a picture of what's to come.

Captivated by the Beauty of the Church

My oldest son loves art. When he first started coloring, he enjoyed a simple container of crayons and markers. These served him well, offering options for drawing monsters, coloring stripes on tigers, and creating rainbows on clean, white paper. To him, these tools were great because he didn't know any other art supplies existed.

Then one snowy morning at home, I pulled a present out of the basement—a children's art kit. This mysterious box had more than crayons. It came filled with pastels, sketch pencils, colored pencils, watercolor paints, and charcoal. When I opened the latch and placed it before him, he squealed with excitement.

He wanted to take full advantage of the art kit, but he quickly realized that these tools (while various and beautiful) were also challenging. As he got the hang of them, creating monsters with textural hair, swiping the sky with brushstrokes of paint, and marking details with tiny pencils, he noticed that they produced richer and lovelier pieces of art. He still uses his crayons and markers, but when that art kit is within reach, it's his palette of choice.

My son's choice of art supplies reminds us of the difference between cultural

JESUS LOVES
HIS BRIDE,
THE CHURCH,
SO MUCH THAT
HE'S COMING
BACK FOR HER

mom tribes and the local church community. Mom tribes offer us good fellowship and practical ideas about everyday life. Like crayons and markers, they work great for many things. No one throws away good crayons! But we'll joyfully reach for the full art kit as we catch God's vision for community in the local church.

A Picture of Gospel Community: Love and Be Loved

As I've processed my youngest son's developmental delays, referring to him as having special needs and seeing him use a wheelchair, I've often wondered where to turn. Online support groups offer helpful and practical anecdotes about kids with various disabilities. Other moms in my town have toddlers who also struggle to walk and talk, and there is wisdom to gain from them as we band together in solidarity. I doubt I'll stop giving them big hugs anytime soon.

But I've also noticed a deep ache in my heart that no special-needs mama can quench. When I know that we have a particularly hard doctor's appointment coming up, my church family prays for us. When I receive hard news, someone from church comes over to cry with me. When I'm worn out from weekly appointments, my church friends encourage me to remember God's faithfulness. This group of people helps me prevail against deep despair and doubt.

In all of this, my husband and I have both learned that God's design for community in the local church doesn't always appear to be the obvious answer for our current need, but it is an abundant provision. When we're willing to be vulnerable about the difficulties of our lives, others can serve us with meals, visits, text messages, and even fits of laughter.

You might be thinking, "That sounds great, but I tried to get involved in my local church and no one returned my text messages. My mom tribe texts me back right away! Besides, there aren't any other young moms at my church. The older couples are completely out of touch and don't seem to care about investing in younger people, and I don't have any margin to get to know people right now."

Maybe you're right. In fact, I'm sure you've noticed completely true things that aren't aligned with God's ideal for church community. No church body full of saints-but-still-sinners will love you perfectly. They might not immediately commiserate when your kids wake up at night, but that's where another wonderful part of being in a local church tribe comes to bear—the part where we learn to love others because we're one in Christ, even when it's not comfortable or convenient for us.

We live out the gospel as we lay down our lives for the love of the saints, holding these fellow partakers of grace in our hearts.[11] The affection of Christ manifested in our lives for our brothers and sisters compels us to pray when we hear they are struggling with a difficult foster care placement. We welcome the single person to our dinner table to laugh and play with our children. We ask the older members of the church community what they've learned about life. We support missionaries and pray for them with our children. In the local church, we learn that "we're bound together by faith, not experience."[12]

God has given us many gracious outlets for relationship and community. These sometimes include like-minded peers, but his most comprehensive, beautiful, helpful, and hopeful design is a living body of believers. It's not just a group of arms (like-minded appendages that imitate the same things); it's a complex living organism where each person brings glory to God and love to others as they serve the head, who is Christ. Mama, enjoy your mom tribe, but find your flourishing, your *primary community*, in the local church.

DISCUSSION QUESTIONS

1. What is your hope for community in motherhood, and how does that picture line up with God's plan for community?

2. Do your heart and actions reflect Christ's heart for his church? Even though it's flawed, what ultimately makes the church beautiful and fruitful?

3. How can you find, commit to, or further invest in your local church community, even in this busy season of motherhood?

---

[11] Philippians 1:7-8.

[12] Dietrich Bonhoeffer, *Life Together* (New York, NY: Harper One, 2009), 39.

THE GOSPEL
AND OUR SERVICE

Laura

Pre-kids, the lasagna would have been entirely homemade. But today it's a jar of marinara, no-boil noodles, and pre-shredded mozzarella cheese. My kids stand on step stools at the kitchen counter, asking to pour the sauce, randomly snapping the dry noodles and watching them fly around the kitchen, and requesting incessantly to stir the cheese mixture. I talk with them about taking turns, not ruining the noodles, and how they can't eat all the cheese—we need to save enough for another family.

Somehow, the lasagna makes it in one piece into the oven, and we start on cookies. These are usually the biggest hurdle in the project. They turn the mixer on and off for me. When it goes on, it usually goes so fast the flour puffs out onto my shirt. Much to their disappointment, I let them have only one cookie each. "They're for the Hardens," I tell them. "Their mommy just had a baby, and this meal helps her care for the rest of her family well."

Once everything is done, we pack up paper plates, juice boxes, a salad-in-a-bag, and a few other items and head to the car. We drive across town to deliver dinner to a family that looks much like ours—they welcomed their fourth child a couple of weeks earlier. As the kids and I walk up the path, they have questions:

"Can we go inside and play? Whose house is this? Why can't we eat the cookies? Can I have a juice box? Why are we here?"

I answer what I can while juggling the meal and the baby, which means I make a couple of trips to and from the car. We ring the doorbell, hand off the meal, and chat with the family for a few minutes. Then we head back to the car and I load up the kids again, only to be met with more questions.

I tell them that sometimes people need extra help. Sometimes it's because hard things come into their lives, like sickness or disability, and sometimes it's because of wonderful things, like childbirth or adoption. I tell them it's because Jesus loved us first that we can love others. That he designed the body of Christ to work that way. That we want to be generous with the good gifts God has given us and use them to bless others.

I say this in imperfect words. I'm interrupted a lot. I fumble and misspeak. The kids are tired because it's nearing naptime. I'm tired because this one thing took all morning and I still have a lot to do today. But I know it's worth it. Because while service with littles in tow is harder than it used to be, I trust that God uses it to plant seeds of generosity, kindness, and selflessness in their lives. I trust that God will use it to help them see how we can be the tangible hands and feet of Christ.

Culture's Message: Stay or Serve, It's One or the Other

In the years of raising small children, you don't have to step outside your door to find needs. They're all around you—the three-foot humans running down your hallways, the four-page hospital bill on your table, and the two-foot laundry pile in your bedroom. The needs are many, they're real, and they're certainly more than you feel you can keep up with.

At the same time, it's clear the rest of the world has needs too. Just turn on the TV, check your cell phone, read a billboard, talk with your neighbor, or listen to your friend's story, and you'll quickly be reminded that help is needed everywhere.

As moms, we tend to handle the needs in two different ways. Some of us want to dive in and try to fix as many things as we can. We understand the needs of the world don't meet themselves, and we are happy to help a noble cause, sometimes so much so it comes at the expense of our family. We soothe the prick in our souls by reminding ourselves that serving others is important. "My husband and children can take care of themselves. If we don't meet the need, who will?"

Plus it feels good to be productive and accomplish something honorable. Serving often yields immediate results, unlike our attention to the never-ending needs of the home. The food pantry is filled, the meal is prepared and delivered, and the event is planned, executed, and completed. And bonus—it's always more fun to serve people who actually seem grateful for our skills and generosity. It's a nice change from having to prompt our children to say thank you every time we hand them a sippy cup of milk.

Others wonder how we as moms can make any difference outside the home when we can't even keep our sink free of dirty dishes. So we keep to ourselves, not daring to look beyond our own domains. The needs are great enough inside our four walls. We tell ourselves, "Babies and toddlers are a lot. Someone else will take care of the needs. Someone else who is passionate about the cause, who has more time, more sleep—they'll do it better anyway."

We find relief in this because getting out of our comfort zone, talking with people we don't know, using a skill we feel we haven't mastered, waking up earlier than we already do…these things are hard. Plus kids are unpredictable, so they can't always come alongside us in service. And frankly, we just want to avoid creating extra work for ourselves. So we ignore the outside needs. If we just pretend they don't exist, we won't have to deal with them, right?

The needs both inside and outside the home are truly great, but the gospel bids us lift our eyes to a greater view than picking just one or the other. Like Jesus charged the disciples, we must keep our lamps burning until his return.[1] We're not called to turn off our lamp when we have children. Nor are we to turn

[1] Luke 12:35.

it on only when we leave the house. We're to keep our fire and teach our children how to burn.

The Gospel Message

CREATION: Created to Serve

Genesis tells us that God placed Adam in the garden to "work it and keep it."[2] In the original Hebrew, the word "work" also means "serve," and it brings with it the idea of serving others, of making oneself a servant. Adam was to serve God by protecting the garden, keeping things in order, and plain ol' hard work. God created Eve to be a "helper,"[3] which means exactly what it sounds like: She offered essential and necessary help with the work God had set before Adam. Adam couldn't do it without her.

At that time, the needs of Eden—the ground to cultivate, the harvest to bring in, and the animals to care for—were many, and Adam and Eve were busy. Because sin hadn't infiltrated the earth yet, they were able to keep up together. Today's desperate needs were in the distant future.

FALL: Bitter Service

Eventually, Adam and Eve doubted the goodness of God's plan for work and service. So they ate of the fruit, hoping it would bring them something better, but it was only bitter. Their doubt pulled them and all of creation into a harsh and broken place. Banished from Eden, for the first time Adam and Eve were unable to complete all the tasks set before them. With sickness, pain, toil, and sweat, the needs were great, and many were left unmet.

Because of the fall, we have orphans and widows. People are poor, hungry, and displaced. We have mental illness, physical illness, broken bones, broken hearts—sin twists and turns its way into every living being. And not only that, sin has crawled its way into the earth, which shudders and groans under the

---

[2] Genesis 2:15.

[3] Genesis 2:18.

WE'RE TO
KEEP OUR
FIRE AND
TEACH OUR
CHILDREN
HOW TO
BURN

weight of the curse—oceans and land, plants and animals all struggling and fighting for survival.

On paper, we wouldn't all be categorized as needy or vulnerable. But the needs don't just live outside our walls; the twisted thread of sin winds its way into our homes too. We bounce between the urgent and the important, neither one receiving the attention it deserves. Our children need us, our yards need us, our schools need us, our laundry rooms need us.

The demands may pull you in so tight, you struggle to look out the window, afraid that the balls you're currently juggling will drop and afraid of what might be asked of you. Sin locks down your heart, so you keep your head low and do only what's necessary, fearful of what you might find if you ever got up the courage to peek outside.

Or you may try to escape your family's incessant needs and dream about making a bigger impact on the world. You push yourself beyond healthy limits, saying yes to every opportunity at the expense of your children, your husband, and your own necessary self-care. You play God, trying to fix the needs of the world, acting like a superhuman when you are simply human.

REDEMPTION: A Servant Sacrifice

But one man was not like the rest of broken humanity. Jesus flipped the world upside down—or rather, right side up. He deserves all our service, yet he came "not to be served but to serve, and to give his life as a ransom for many."[4] Jesus is the King of the universe. He speaks, and the wind obeys; he touches, and the blind are healed; he walks, and the water holds him; he sleeps, and even then all things are held together in him. This all-powerful, all-sufficient, all-knowing God-man came to serve us. It's mind-boggling, really.

As Jesus walked this earth, the needs were great. People came to him one after another—in the temple, on the roadside, in the fields, on the lake, through a roof. Rather than turning aside and looking away, Jesus met them head-on,

---

[4] Matthew 20:28; Mark 10:45.

revealing his generous heart and extending grace, mercy, tenderness, and overflowing kindness. He loved the needy, the vulnerable, the unlovable. Ultimately, Christ served us in the greatest way of all, dying a torturous death on a Roman cross, giving his very life for us, the needy, dependent, and broken.[5]

Even now, Christ continues to serve us.[6] In his power and following his example, we model his heart of love for helpless people, serving even when it's costly or uncomfortable. In him we have the Holy Spirit,[7] who gives us new eyes for the lost, a soft heart for the vulnerable, courage for the unknown, and perseverance when life gets hard. In our service, we worship, showing gratitude for all that has been done for us. The more we depend on him and recognize our limits, the more he shows himself to be sufficient.

CONSUMMATION: The Servant King

It's not just now that Christ is our servant; he will continue to serve at the second coming and for eternity. As Jesus talked with his disciples about being ready for his return, he told them he would continue to serve them when they joined him in paradise.[8] The same Christ who returns with armies and fire[9] will continue to serve us, even at the end of the age.

Serving Others So We Can Disciple our Children

I saw her coming down the hallway before she saw me. I had a feeling if we met, she'd ask me to do something I didn't want to do. As our paths crossed, we greeted each other, made some small talk—and then it came: "Are you able to come to next week's event? I'm looking for one more person to work the welcome table."

I really didn't want to. It meant I would have to come 45 minutes early, be

---

[5] John 13:14.

[6] Hebrews 7:25.

[7] John 14:26.

[8] Luke 12:37.

[9] 1 Thessalonians 1:8; Revelation 19:14.

chipper and energetic when all I felt was tired, and miss a chance to hang out with my friends beforehand. I would be peeling and sticking name tags on sweaters and telling people where the bathrooms were—not necessarily my idea of a good use of babysitter time.

I agreed, but I wished she had asked someone else.

Isn't that how many of us feel about service? We hope and pray someone else will fill in the gaps. Or maybe you're the opposite—maybe you're the type of person who feels burdened to fill in the gaps, saying yes to each opportunity even when you know you don't have the capacity.

Whatever direction you swing, the Bible offers hope. For believers, engaging in service is not optional. Christ commands us to love him and love others,[10] and that includes serving the vulnerable, the needy, the stranger, and the hard to love. This doesn't say we must have a degree in counseling to talk with a mom next door or a hefty bank account to provide for a local ministry, and we don't have to be a "kid person" to work in the nursery at church. Yet at the same time, as moms, we have a critical ministry opportunity with our children and families. This means, at times, we have to say no to valuable or worthwhile opportunities and causes in order to care well for those God has placed closest to us.

And so we minister to our family *and* to those outside of our family. We cannot have one without the other. To live out our calling as followers of Christ is to show our children that loving God means loving others. It takes both. These little years are a training ground for our children, a launchpad for them to begin to understand what a lifetime of godly service and ministry looks like. Much of that will happen by your example as you show your children what loving others looks like—both inside and outside your family.

Burn for the Gospel

The great thing about ministry is that it can take many forms. Sometimes the kids help us. (Okay, they *sort of* help us.) Maybe we watch a friend's children

---

[10] Luke 10:27.

LOVING GOD
MEANS
LOVING OTHERS

while she goes to an appointment, we drop off diapers at a local women's shelter, we work on our church's marketing materials during naptime, or we care for kids in the local foster care system. Sometimes we leave our kids behind as we head out to serve at our local church, counsel at a crisis pregnancy center, or attend a service project through our place of work. We can hope and pray that over time, as our children see a mother who pours out her life for others, they will catch a vision of what it means to burn for the gospel.

The hard part is, no one can tell you how much service is right for you. The balance is different for everyone and is only found by searching your heart and submitting your time and desires to God through prayer. If your tendency is to avoid service to those outside of your immediate family, remember God's heart for the dependent and needy, and trust Him (the ultimate servant-leader) to supply all you need when you say yes in faith to the needs of your neighbors and church family. If your tendency is to be the first to sign up while your children are asking when they can spend time with you, trust that God is the one who ultimately meets all needs. You can say no to some things so you can invest well in the lives of those who live in your home.

You may need to pull back, or you may need to jump in deeper. There will be seasons where your schedule is filled with all different types of service, and there will be other seasons when talking to and encouraging your neighbor after work is truly all you can manage. In all of this, your lamp is burning. Because what God asks for is faithfulness in everyday moments and living out his commandments, not a certain quantity of service projects or perfect execution of the task. He asks you to see the needs all around you and then to use the good gifts he has equipped you with to serve others as he has served you.

DISCUSSION QUESTIONS

1. Do you tend to lean toward serving your family or serving others? How do your natural tendencies align to God's call to service?

2. You're not made righteous by your actions. How does knowing

this free you from trying to earn favor or feeling burdened when serving?

3. What are some specific ways you can model Christ's life of service to others today? What would it look like to use that service as a training ground for your children?

THE GOSPEL
AND OUR SELF-CARE

Emily

As newlyweds, our first major purchase was a top-of-the-line laptop. It was our most expensive possession aside from our aging vehicles. Shortly into my experience as a laptop owner, I started to receive update notifications in the middle of answering an email or making a purchase. It felt so inconvenient to reboot the computer in the middle of a task, so instead, I clicked "remind me tomorrow."

The reminders built up for months and then years until eventually they went from inconvenient to disabling. When Laura and I needed to record a podcast over a video call, my computer froze and shut down. When I needed to access Microsoft Word to work on a piece of writing, my cursor stopped functioning. When I needed to upload some pictures for a Christmas gift, my browser window gave me an error message.

Eventually, the computer stopped functioning altogether. Our negligence (um…*my* negligence) to complete the regularly suggested updates probably had something to do with its ultimate demise.

Eight years into marriage, we purchased another top-of-the-line laptop, and this time, I was determined to take care of it. So two days later, when the little "you have an update" notification appeared on my screen, I clicked "update now" instead of "remind me tomorrow." This new perspective on laptop stewardship came from the realization that there was no avoiding maintenance.

Unfortunately I've learned this lesson the hard way in motherhood too. Much like the way I treated my first laptop, I often see my human needs and think, "I don't have any time for rest right now. Maybe tomorrow." I believe I'm helping my family by giving them more of me immediately, but in the end I'm very little help. An empty cup, I have nothing to pour into those I'm called to serve.

Culture's Message: If I Just Had More Time for Me

Everyone knows that moms are worn down and would benefit from taking better care of their own needs. But the world tells us our needs are rooted in the demands of our role. We earn "me time" through our dishwashing, laundry folding, hours spent playing trains with our toddlers, and laying down our desires to care for our family. We need because they need.

Self-care, or "me time," includes the things we do to care for our mind, body, and heart. This might include reading a novel, taking a bath, exercising regularly, splurging financially, keeping a gratitude journal, baking, maintaining a special diet, walking around the store alone, having a girl's day at the spa, taking a nap, traveling, or even pursuing a hobby in a meaningful way. Some of these strategies are more need-based, and others more comfort-based. Methods of self-care are deeply personal and vary widely.

Our hearts are prone to thinking that if we just had more "me time"—hiring extra childcare so we could complete our workouts, eat our vegetables, wear our makeup, take our naps, and drink our lattes in peace—maybe motherhood wouldn't feel so hard. Maybe we wouldn't feel like we're drowning.

But as any mom who's tried to strike the perfect "me time" balance can tell you, it can be as elusive as trying to hold on to a fistful of sand. Many moms have discovered that no person (however well cared for) can find satisfying soul-rest in carefully crafted circumstances.

The Gospel Message

CREATION: Created with Needs

Our culture tells us we need self-care because our kids need our care, but the creation account tells us we need care because God made us that way. Adam and Eve had bountiful provision in Eden, but they still had ongoing needs. They had to eat. They had to sleep. They needed fellowship with God and each other. Needs existed before the fall, so they are part of God's good design. Then and now, they remind us of our limitations—that God is God and we are not. We're fragile creatures with an invincible Creator.

Additionally, God made us with the propensity to enjoy. Beyond just meeting our basic physical needs, he gives us food worth feasting on and relationships worth celebrating. Life has moments of complete beauty. No wonder we desire to have our needs met *and then some.*

FALL: Finding Ways to Fill Our Needs

Even though God provided for the needs and pleasure of his people in Eden, Satan stoked a flame of dissatisfaction. He questioned God's boundaries and encouraged Eve to become more like God in his wisdom and knowledge.[1]

When Adam and Eve sinned, disobeying God by desiring to be in his place, they experienced a totally new feeling—the need for a covering. Seeking to take care of this themselves, they fashioned insufficient clothing from fig leaves and hid from God in shame.[2] But as would be the case for all future sinners, sufficient coverage would require the shedding of innocent blood.[3] And only God could do it.

We are like Adam and Eve in their sin when we pridefully try to live beyond our designated limitations. We try to be like God—all-wise, all-sustaining, sleep-foregoing, self-sacrificing superhumans for those we love, thinking that

---

[1] Genesis 3:5.

[2] Genesis 3:7.

[3] Genesis 3:21.

we're different somehow. Or maybe we're like Adam and Eve as we try to find solutions to our needs and wants apart from God's provision. We avoid the pleasure of soul-rest while leveraging every coping mechanism we can—gulping the wine, scheduling the hair appointment, going to the gym. Instead of enjoying things as good gifts from the Lord, we see them as possible solutions for our deeper weariness.

But the truth is, we can't drink our way to soul-level satisfaction, and we can't dress well enough to appear blameless before the throne. Even if we could be healthy and happy in this life, our efforts could never pay our eternal debt for our sin against God or give us everlasting life.

REDEMPTION: Needs Met in Christ

In Jesus' wilderness temptation, Satan twisted God's word again, hoping Jesus would accept quick-fix solutions to meet his needs. Even though Jesus was hungry and tired, he believed and obeyed God, trusting his Father's provision.[4]

In his life and ministry, Jesus set an example for self-care by framing all his human needs and wants in the context of his Father's will. Jesus took breaks and made time for eating with friends, sleeping peacefully, communing with God, and enjoying relationships. Sometimes he confused his disciples, who went looking for him when there seemed to be more work at hand.[5] Why was Jesus able to rest when it looked like he needed to work? He trusted God.

And sometimes Jesus confused his disciples by serving others when it was his turn to be served. Even when Jesus was hungry, uncomfortable, or exhausted, he stooped to wash people's feet. He still laid hands on the hurting. Why was Jesus able to lay down his rights when it looked like he needed a break? He trusted God.

We continually see Jesus faithfully accomplishing the will of the Father within the limitations of a human body.

---

[4] Matthew 4:1-11.

[5] Mark 1:35-39.

Jesus shows us that self-care isn't about perfect balance, earthly happiness, having everything we want, or even holding on to our lives. Instead it's about losing our lives in faithful obedience. We can follow his example and turn to him in our need for basics and beauty because he understands and provides us a Helper.

CONSUMMATION: Final and Full Rest Is Coming

Someday, when God's kingdom comes into fullness, we won't feel overwhelmed by the needs of little ones, the large piles of laundry, or our sleep deprivation. We won't feel sad about missed opportunities to bake fresh loaves of bread or tend to our garden. Instead we'll rest because we have no reason to hide from the throne. As our deepest needs are fully met in Christ and our loveliest joys found in him, we'll praise God forever.

Self-Care—Planned For yet Fallible

In my transition from four to five children, for a moment I thought, "I've got this." From my previous experience, I knew I needed a plan to steward my mind, body, and heart for service to God. But many times and in many ways, I stumbled.

In the first several months, I tried to ignore my needs. I could shower, care for my baby, have my children home for most of the day, get my son to therapy appointments, complete my Bible study, work on the Risen Motherhood ministry, volunteer at church, and stay up late to watch Netflix with my husband all while getting less-than-ideal sleep. I knew it wasn't sustainable, but I thought, "Hey, remind me tomorrow. I'll get God's help when I'm even more worn down."

After several months, I started feeling overwhelmed. I found myself daydreaming about an easier life, where I could spend more time doing what I wanted and less time wiping bottoms, cleaning dishes, and training little sinners. I wondered if I should fake an illness just to get some extra rest.

So after I waved the white flag, my husband and I committed to a new plan. I would exercise, eat better, take time on the weekends for rest, get support with childcare, and enroll our twins in preschool. I would say yes to practical solutions for help around the house and take time to read my Bible in silence. In that season, I also said no to new church ministry opportunities, nonessential house projects, and even cooking elaborate meals.

All of this helped for a while. I felt much better—less irritable with the kids, happier, and more excited and hopeful. Then some rough weeks arrived. Due to ongoing illness, travel, weather, and work, my carefully crafted self-care routine crumbled. At one point, I went nearly five days without leaving our house or cracking open my Bible. I needed to find a way to rejoice and rest in the middle of hard things.

In that season, I learned some critical things about self-care and the issues we face as moms:

Pride often keeps us from seeking God in our need. My self-sufficient attitude caused me to ignore my limitations, but God is able to "make all grace abound" to me so I can do his work through his equipping.[6] We can come to him in need, humility, and weakness.

Self-care strategies are limited. A long vacation might have helped (like my daydreams promised), but for how long? More time for my hobbies would have given me time away, but those effects are temporary. We will always need more, new, and different types of self-care. God provides the only unlimited well of refreshment in Christ.

We can't fix our hope for happiness in self-care strategies. Sickness happens, husbands have unexpected work conflicts, clouds dump snow, babysitters cancel, and people still need us. In those times—and when we're totally exhausted— what should we do?

Hope Is Found in the Unfailing Christ

Just as my laptop's customer care instructions don't guarantee my device will always function properly, self-care strategies don't promise us an easier life.

---

[6] 2 Corinthians 9:8.

GOD CARES
FOR US WHEN
WE CAN'T CARE
FOR OURSELVES

Computers break down because of attacks from viruses and damage from spills. They can come straight from the manufacturer with built-in faults. As participants in the great redemptive story (not the authors of it), we don't have control over all the factors that influence physical, spiritual, and emotional health. Despite our lack of control over circumstances, God offers us rest in the here and now through Christ.

One of my favorite pictures of this in the Bible is in the life of the apostle Paul as he faces weariness and discouragement in ministry. He writes about his experience (one that would challenge all our modern mom expectations about the things we think we need to be happy and cared for):

> We have this treasure in jars of clay, to show that the surpassing power belongs to God and not to us. We are afflicted in every way, but not crushed; perplexed, but not driven to despair; persecuted, but not forsaken; struck down, but not destroyed; always carrying in the body the death of Jesus, so that the life of Jesus may also be manifested in our bodies (2 Corinthians 4:7-10).

As fragile, human jars of clay, our hope isn't in our ideal self-care routine or in the satiation of our needs, but in the treasure we carry—Christ in us. Only in him can we endure the present moment with rejoicing instead of despair, security instead of fear. God promises that although things will be hard in this life from never-ending demands and strife, he will sustain us in the most important way to show his surpassing power.

He allows hardship in our lives so we can reveal the life of Jesus in our everyday circumstances. When the kids are bawling over who knows what, when we haven't exercised in weeks, when we can't even remember what a "girlfriend" is, when we haven't had a haircut in a year, when our stack of books to read is sky-high, when our husband doesn't come home until 11:00 p.m., when our baby wakes up five times a night, or when our heart feels like it can't limp through another day—we can sing "It Is Well with My Soul" and mean it. We can do what makes us happiest, which is living in obedience to God as we love others in his name, even (and especially) when that means forsaking something we'd like to have for ourselves.

In many cases, self-care is wise, good, and important. But only God's care and sustaining power can shape us into the image of Christ through the Holy Spirit, with or without our self-care strategies. Whether we're like Paul in prison (suffering and struggling for the gospel), a modern-day persecuted Christian, or a tired mom in a difficult season, God cares for us when we can't care for ourselves. He sees the end. He gives us some rest now, and we look forward to truer, better, and final rest to come.

> *If you think you might be struggling with postpartum depression, postpartum OCD, anxiety disorder, or something similar, please tell someone and reach out to a professional for help.*

DISCUSSION QUESTIONS

1. What's your ideal version of self-care? Do you have enough margin in your life to engage in it right now? If not, what barriers do you face?

2. How do you react when your self-care strategies fall through? What does that reveal about your heart? If you rarely take enough time for rest or self-care, what might that reveal about your worship and beliefs?

3. Even if you don't have time for traditional methods of self-care, have you stopped to pray and trust God with your deepest needs? How is he sustaining you?

16

THE GOSPEL AND OUR CHILDREN WITH DIFFERENCES

Laura

Some moments are frozen in time, never to be forgotten. One of mine occurred in a small, white doctor's office, filled too full with paperwork, charts, graphs, whispers, long pauses, five adults, and a single baby. My baby.

"Will she walk?" I asked.

"We can be hopeful," the lead doctor responded.

"Will she talk?" I asked.

"We can be hopeful," she repeated.

"We just don't have any idea how she'll turn out," a genetic counselor added.

I looked at my daughter, sleeping in my arms. Words wouldn't come. I knew I should be asking questions, but I didn't know what to ask. So instead I hid my tears as I adjusted her blanket, smoothing the pink, peony-printed fabric over her tiny legs. My husband asked a few more questions, but mostly we just sat silently in the uncomfortable molded red chairs, stunned and shocked.

As we drove home, we called our closest family members, who had been praying for the appointment. We picked up our older children from a friend's house. I made dinner. Our hearts felt smashed into a million tiny pieces, yet life

173

went on like normal. My husband put the big kids down for bed, I nursed the baby, we watched a show, I washed the dishes.

I couldn't keep my thoughts from reaching far into the future, wondering what our lives would look like. "Will she walk? Will she talk?" These questions swirled in my mind like the dish soap in the water. My chest felt tight, my legs felt weak, my heart fought for hope. I felt overcome by despair and grief for my daughter, for my family, for me. As my tears spilled into the kitchen sink, I cried, "I can't do this. I need you, God. I don't know what to do!"

Nothing magically changed in that moment. I still felt grief and inability. I still had so many questions. But in the waves of fear and sorrow that crashed against my heart, I clung to the hope of the gospel.

Culture's Message: You Are the Only Hope

No one goes into motherhood expecting their child to have disabilities, health needs, behavioral issues. No mom expects her child will require medical interventions. But many moms will face unexpected news about their child. For some women, the diagnosis finally explains their questions and concerns and almost comes as a relief. Now they know what they're dealing with and can find answers. For others, it's the last thing they saw coming, and it's paralyzing and numbing.

But either way, learning your child has differences—whether it's getting a hearing aid or glasses for the first time, learning about a food allergy or sensory processing disorder, or receiving a diagnosis of a developmental delay or disability—can feel difficult, painful, and even devastating.

The world comforts mothers by telling them to be thankful they live in the twenty-first century and have access to advanced medical care. Whether it's glasses or a wheelchair, a simple facial cosmetic surgery or a vital, life-saving, open-heart surgery, if you have enough money, connections, and motivation, you can change whatever the future holds through technology and capable doctors and therapists.

"Put your hope in your care team," culture tells you. "They know what to do."

In addition to getting their children the best medical care, the best moms are the "mama bears." A mom must be her child's best advocate. Research to the end of the internet and back and become an expert in the child's specific care needs. Tweak their diet, use special oils, try a new clinical study, do the home therapies perfectly every day. Test new equipment, have them take special vitamins each morning, and be sure to massage the correct parts of their feet.

"You are their hope," the world tells you. "Their outcome and development are direct reflections of your abilities."

The pressure put on a parent to be the answer to their child's need is crushing. No mere human can possibly keep up, yet a mom continues to be fed the lie that if she finds the issue early enough, if she cares for it diligently enough, if she works on it hard enough, she can control the outcome of her child's future. Our hope, tied to our imperfect efforts, imperfect doctors, and imperfect circumstances, fades and brightens according to our child's development. Some days we're elated; some days we're devastated. Most days it's a bit of both.

We should be thankful for brilliant doctors and therapists, value the amazing advancements of medicine and medical equipment over the years, and be strong advocates for the children in our care. But still, we can't control our children's future. When we are given a difficult diagnosis, we are told to put our hope in our own or others' abilities. But as limited humans, we will fail.

The gospel gives us a better hope. One that doesn't rest on our own merits and capabilities. It is a hope that fed 5,000 with just five loaves and two fish. Made the lame walk. Healed barren wombs. Split seas. Raised dry bones to life. Cared for the smallest sparrow. It is a hope that brings our eyes above our current view to see a bigger story at work.

The Gospel Message

CREATION: Life with the Source of Hope

When God created humans for the first time, their bodies were perfectly formed.[1] Blood pressures stayed level, heartbeats were in rhythm, bones were strong and straight, and the synapses of the brain transmitted flawlessly. Disability, illness, and medical care didn't exist, as Adam and Eve enjoyed able bodies that worked and rested in the garden without so much as a paper cut.

In Eden, our first parents had daily fellowship with the Creator and Sustainer of their bodies. They walked and talked with their source of hope, confident in God and his ways and the life he had designed for them.

FALL: Hopeless Living

When Adam and Eve sinned, they were banished from Eden. As the cherubim and flaming sword turned to and fro to guard the garden,[2] God sent Adam and Eve out to endure toil, pain, and strife.[3] For the first time, they knew the sting of a scraped knee, felt their vision dim as they grew older, and got a cough during a cold.

The fall brought to light the frailty of the human body. With it came sickness, disease, dysfunction, and disability. Sometimes it's from the moment of conception, sometimes it develops over time, sometimes it's in an instant. No matter how they come, the effects of the fall are revealed.

Just as Eve ate of the fruit, looking for a better hope than her God, we grasp for hope anywhere we think we can find it because we doubt a good God could allow suffering. Usually, we muster hope in ourselves—like Eve, craving control of the future, believing we can muscle our way to healing. We tell ourselves we are our child's hope for success. So we draw our swords and prepare for battle, ready to fight to the death (or until the bank account is emptied and our options exhausted). As we do, we cross our fingers and hope for the best. Progress ebbs and flows. When one problem is taken care of, another one crops up. Sometimes, there is no solution, so we learn to live in a new way.

Because our hope is built on shifting sand, our hearts are in constant

---

[1] Genesis 1:27.

[2] Genesis 3:24.

[3] Genesis 3:23.

turmoil, swaying between grief and delight, our attitude and perspective dependent on an ever-moving target. We are exhausted, frustrated, and joyless. We cannot count on our own best efforts, the top medical care, or even our child's progress—and soon it begins to feel as though we have no hope at all in this life.

REDEMPTION: A Living Hope

Amid the most devastating event for all mankind—Adam and Eve's rejection of God—God offered hope. As God unleashes the curse on the earth, there is a promising, pregnant phrase that changes everything: "I will put enmity between you and the woman, and between your offspring and her offspring; he shall bruise your head, and you shall bruise his heel."[4]

Hope. Not to be realized in that moment, but a promise for the future. God doesn't whisk away the effects of the fall, rescuing them immediately. Instead he takes his time breathing life into death. He banishes Adam and Eve east of the garden, allowing them to live and feel the painful repercussions of the fall. As they went, they clung to God's promise that someday Satan and sin will be crushed by a son of Eve.

Adam and Eve never met their Rescuer while they lived on Earth—and Adam lived more than 900 years![5] But they lived with expectant hope in God's promise to redeem them. Each night as they watched the sun set to the west—toward Eden—they probably grieved their old lives. But they didn't grieve without hope. They believed and trusted that one day they would return to an even better Eden.

Their hope wasn't some wishy-washy, possibly, maybe-this-will-happen hope, but a sure and confident hope that something *will* happen in the future. Their hope was a person, but not just any regular person—it was a hope in a perfect person, Jesus Christ. On this side of the cross, we know he came and

---

[4] Genesis 3:15.

[5] Genesis 5:3-4.

fulfilled the prophecy that Adam and Eve's ears heard, crushing the serpent's head by dying and rising again on the third day.[6] We still live in the in-between, waiting for the full consummation of God's plan, when we will enter a more perfect paradise than Eden. But we live today with the hope that this life is not all there is. There is a greater purpose for what we experience.

CONSUMMATION: Eternal Life with Eternal Hope

Someday we will live alongside our Hope again. When God brings about the restoration of all things, we will never again feel the grief, pain, and sorrow of the fall. "He will wipe away every tear from their eyes, and death shall be no more, neither shall there be mourning, nor crying, nor pain anymore, for the former things have passed away."[7] Oh, what a promise to take hope in!

On that day, all disabilities and differences will be fully healed. No more medicines, surgeries, therapies, or appointments. No more late-night fears of how the other children will accept your child, worrying if you're doing enough, saying enough, paying enough. You'll no longer have to weigh the options for care and the risks of the potential side effects. There will be no more need for doctors or nurses because the Great Healer will walk among us.

Hope in the Purpose, Not the Cause

"I…I did have some sushi once while I was pregnant. And this was the first pregnancy I used a pregnancy pillow. Could that have done it?" I hesitantly whispered these things to my husband, wracking my brain for how my daughter could have ended up with such a rare diagnosis. I did the same thing when my son got glasses, when he had multiple eye surgeries and therapy, and when we learned he would struggle with vision issues his entire life. And I did it when my middle child had a speech delay and we learned she had hearing difficulties.

"What did I do wrong?"

---

[6] Genesis 3:15.

[7] Revelation 21:4.

"Is this my fault?"

"How did this happen?"

"*Why* did this happen?"

No matter when or how it happens, knowing your child will have a difference from their regularly developing peers brings pain, grief, and a desperate mother's cry of "Why, God? What do I do now?"

This question is normal, and it is okay to ask God this. The Bible does not shy away from these difficult questions. I take great comfort in that.

The disciples even asked this concerning a blind man: "Who sinned, this man or his parents, that he was born blind?"[8] They assumed it must have been the man's sin, or possibly his parents'. Surely it was someone's fault. But Jesus says something no one expects: "It was not that this man sinned, or his parents, but that the works of God might be displayed in him."[9] He essentially tells the disciples, "It's not because of their sin. Now stop focusing on the cause and start focusing on the purpose."

"Why did this happen?"

So God gets more glory.

If you are a mother facing the challenges of a child with differences, there is a purpose: God is working in your child's life and through their challenges to display his glory—and he is working in you too. The "works of God" are not just displayed in the person who is differently abled; the works of God are also shown through you as you care for them day after day. As you show mercy while you rock them for the seventh time in the middle of the night. As you are patient and kind amid erratic or unusual behaviors in public. As you speak of God's good grace to you when others ask how you do it.

The way you respond to and interact with your child's disability, illness, or behaviors has a deeper meaning. As you navigate diagnosis with a hope in God, even amid questions, misunderstandings, and sorrow, you are displaying

---

[8] John 9:2.

[9] John 9:3.

the life-giving, hope-filling, grace-saturating, compassion-spreading, heart-rearranging, glory-bursting, sin-expelling works of God for all to see.

A Hope That Sanctifies

Difficulty and questions have a way of pressing down hard on unbelief, revealing our doubts, our fears, our bitterness, and the true nature of our faith. We want quick fixes to our problems, but God gives slow solutions—because we're slow learners. God isn't asking you to close your eyes, shoot from the hip, and hope for the best as you navigate the deep waters of your child's care. He also doesn't promise to take away the oceans in front of you. But he does promise to be with you the entire time: "Fear not, for I am with you."[10]

Struggle and patient endurance bring sanctification. They force us to look beyond ourselves and our circumstances and decide if we really believe what he says is true:

"We know that for those who love God all things work together for good, for those who are called according to his purpose."[11]

"He preserves the lives of his saints."[12]

"This light momentary affliction is preparing for us an eternal weight of glory beyond all comparison."[13]

"I will strengthen you, I will help you, I will uphold you with my righteous right hand."[14]

"I will not remove from him my steadfast love or be false to my faithfulness."[15]

"Behold, I am making all things new."[16]

"I am making all things new"—if you are like me, you are desperately longing

---

[10] Isaiah 41:10.

[11] Romans 8:28.

[12] Psalm 97:10.

[13] 2 Corinthians 4:17.

[14] Isaiah 41:10.

[15] Psalm 89:33.

[16] Revelation 21:5.

WHILE WE
WAIT,
WE WAIT
WITH
HOPE

for the day when God will make that promise true for your child. But this should be the cry of your heart for yourself too. Just as your child has a deeper need than their different-ability, so too do you have a deep need for the healing of your heart. We are often tempted to place our hope in therapy progress, a new statistic, how well we advocate for medical care, or if we remember the medicine. But because of Christ, our hope can finally find rest in our unchanging God—in his perfect plan and the faithfulness of his Word.

Preach this truth to yourself every day. The moment you think you have it down pat, you'll forget. Since you're human like me, I know you have a short, stumpy memory. Wake up and remind yourself of the story. Tell yourself of the Rock of Ages. The pillar of cloud and fire. The potter. The burning bush. The one on the white horse. Repeat the gospel to yourself as you face new challenges, discover new questions, celebrate new accomplishments, and experience new hardships.

Wherever you are at in the journey with your child, cling to true, lasting hope and believe in God's promises. Even when you don't understand, remind yourself that there is a greater purpose at work. Trust in God's long game to grow you up in faith as he slowly presses truth into your soul. Display the works of God to those in your life, living by faith and with hope in God's big story coming to completion—knowing that the sun will not always set on Eden.

While we wait, we wait with hope.

DISCUSSION QUESTIONS

1. If you are a mother of a child with differences, where do you tend to place your hope? If you are a friend of a mother in that situation, where do you encourage her to place her hope? How does this align with where the gospel tells us to place our hope?

2. God promises to use our suffering for our sanctification and to draw us closer to himself. How does this give you hope and

encouragement when you receive a challenging diagnosis? In what ways is God making you new?

3. How does the gospel bid you to display the works of God to those around you, using your unique situation to show the deep joy you have in Christ?

THE GOSPEL AND
OUR SCHOOLING CHOICES

Emily

With an ideal picture of our family in mind and a homeschool curriculum on the shelf, I thought I had the next 20 years figured out. Schooling at home would be a hard road, but if we cared enough, we could make it work. Right?

Fast-forward a year, and God's direction for our lives challenged my plans. After a stressful move, a difficult diagnosis for our youngest child, the task of parenting rambunctious twin boys through toddlerhood, and looking ahead to the birth of our fifth child, I discovered my limitations. During those days, focusing our time on school felt impossible. We made our best effort to faithfully educate our kids in the truth as God tasks us in his Word, but it didn't feel like enough if we weren't schooling in my ideal way.

When my husband brought up the prospect of sending our oldest child to early kindergarten, I initially resisted. I worried that sending him off to school was akin to sending him down the wrong path for his entire life.

My husband smiled graciously. "We need help next year. Let's just take it one year at a time."

I labored over the decision and felt guilt, but oddly, it wasn't because the school was a poor option. (It was a great school!) I struggled because it meant changing course and potentially looking weak and embarrassed in front of others. I struggled because I wanted to display all the strength and wisdom of my parenting as I persevered in this decision, even if it was hard. I wasn't worried about our schooling choice; I was worried about my righteousness.

Culture's Message: Your Schooling Choices Determine the Future

When we evaluate school choices (if we even have the luxury of options), we often see a big intersection. The signs above the roads appear to point to different places.

- Send your child to this school, and they're headed to an Ivy League university, a six-figure income, and an impressive professional career.

- Send your child to that school, and they'll have great evangelism opportunities, go to an in-state university, and a get job in their hometown.

- Keep your child at home for school, and they'll develop a love of learning, a life of godliness, and a future as a faithful member of a local church.

Of course, these are stereotypes. All of us see different paths with different outcomes, but the illustration holds true. We imagine if we can just send our kids down the right path, we can control their destination. We also like to believe we can never change paths again—and some (we fear) might be headed toward a cliff.

Our own life experiences, our community, and the messages of the world reinforce this mentality. We look down the street and see our neighbors happily sending their kids to the bus stop, and we fear our homeschooled children will miss out on something important. We have dinner with our homeschooling friends and feel sad about our own choice for public school when we hear how much time they spend together as a family. We crunch all the numbers, hoping that if we can just fit the private school of our dreams into the budget, then our child will be set for life. Memories of our own childhoods remind us of how this or that schooling experience impacted our friendships, our faith, and our future. We are duped into thinking there is a special formula for evaluating all the possibilities, spinning the wheel, and coming up with a foolproof solution for our own kids. With so much weight on the one decision-making moment for school choice, sometimes we forget God's sovereignty over the whole intersection.

The Gospel Message

CREATION: Two Paths

In the beginning, God created the heavens and the earth.[1] Whatever he spoke came into being.[2] No one instructed him, explained the science, or provided him the materials. He needed no extra-special wisdom or revelation. From the triune God alone came the ideas, the means, the power, and the product—and right away, we see God has all knowledge and is Lord of all knowledge. He sees the best decisions that lead to the best outcomes. There is nothing any creature needs to teach him.

Into this world, Adam and Eve are created as image-bearers of the God who wields his knowledge to achieve his own ends. He presents them with two paths, showing them the way to life or death.[3]

FALL: The Path of Pride and Control

But Eve, tempted by the serpent to control her own destiny, ate the forbidden fruit. Instead of taking God's path for life, she defied him and attempted

---

[1] Genesis 1:1.

[2] Genesis 1:3.

[3] Genesis 2:15-17.

to live outside of God's way.[4] When she realized she'd defied God's path for her life, she hid with Adam in shame.[5]

Her pride—her desire to gain access to God's position, becoming like him in knowledge and power—trickles down to us today. As Eve wanted to control her life, so we desire to control ours and our children's. We think that as we stand at the intersection of school choice, we can consider all the factors and pick one that gives them life. We leverage education for their position, power, status, financial stability, and sometimes even their salvation.

If we can't send our child down our ideal path for schooling, our shame-filled hearts well up with anxiety. Sometimes we feel embarrassed because while our peers evaluate all their options, our budget and work limit our choices. Our insecurity might also lead us to deliver sarcastic judgment on families who can send their kids down the school path that we wanted. We hope school choice doesn't matter *that* much—kids are kids, and they'll turn out fine if we have good intentions. Right?

Or when we *can* provide our ideal school choice, we are prone to judgment in another way, thinking that if other parents could just get their act together and try harder, care more, and sacrifice (as we have), then they would be on the best path (like ours). Maybe they just need to quit their jobs, crunch the numbers harder, or get the training to care for their child's needs themselves.

Each person (regardless of their education philosophy) is prone to sinful heart attitudes as they consider school choices and evaluate other families according to their standards. We're all prone to letting our school choices give us an exaggerated sensation of power and control over the future of our children, even if they do have some influence.

REDEMPTION: The Narrow Path

It's a great thing to desire a good future for our children, just as God does for

---

[4] Genesis 3:4.

[5] Genesis 3:10.

his own children. He provides us the ability to use wisdom as the Holy Spirit helps us apply his Word to our circumstances as we trust Christ.

King Solomon illustrates the value of wise choices in the book of Ecclesiastes, acknowledging that wisdom is much better than foolishness.[6] Wisdom can yield good experiences, investments, relationships, and even enjoyment of God. But wise choices have limitations because they come from the minds of fallen sinners. We don't have the infinite wisdom and knowledge of God, and we don't have sovereignty over all outcomes. King Solomon reminds us that everyone—the well-educated and the uneducated—will face the same death.[7] Even he, with the gift of exceptional human wisdom, walked in sin. His life shows us that in everything, we must care about imaging Christ as we apply wisdom.[8]

Scripture helps us see that while wise school choices are good, a method or institution doesn't have the power to send our children down the right path for eternity. For that, there is only one answer: Our children must enter through the narrow gate, and we can't make them enter through ideally crafted life circumstances.[9]

Only in Christ can our children find eternal life, true wisdom, gospel purpose, kingdom success, and lasting joy. We get the privilege and joy of pointing them down his path regardless of the school choice we make. We trust the God of creation, who spoke life into existence and sent a Savior to rescue his people, to find his sheep and bring them into the fold.[10] Salvation belongs to the Lord, and there is no other name (or ideal school choice) given to mankind by which we are saved.[11]

---

[6] Ecclesiastes 2:13.

[7] Ecclesiastes 2:14.

[8] 1 Corinthians 2:16.

[9] Matthew 7:13-14.

[10] John 10:16.

[11] Psalm 3:8; Acts 4:12.

CONSUMMATION: A Hope Beyond the Next School Year

Jesus tells us in Revelation that he's returning soon.[12] When he comes, he will gather those who walked the same path he did.[13] Some of the saints who join him eternally will have been homeschooled, some will have attended private schools or public schools, and some will have experienced all of the above. Some will have Ivy League educations, and some will be illiterate. But all will have walked through the narrow gate of his salvation. This is the path that really matters.

As we picture a schooling path for our children, we don't just hope for ideal teachers—we pray those teachers (and everyone else we encounter there) will become brothers and sisters in Christ, worshipping beside us on the new earth.

Pointing Our Children Down His Path

This is not a chapter about what schooling method you should choose. You might have planned to send your child off to public school this year, but instead you're going to homeschool. Or maybe you need to keep your child enrolled at the local school and not change your original plans. Your kids might need to be involved in different schools for different reasons. My sister, whatever circumstances are in your life, and whatever options are available to you as you read this, I hope this chapter gives you freedom and reminds you of your God-given task.

Let's all take a deep breath and put down our swords, expectations, fears, and assumptions. As we tuck our weapons away, let's think about the impact our family culture—the "characteristic features of our everyday existence"[14]— has on our children.

Your school choices matter, but Deuteronomy 6:7-9 also insinuates that all the patterns of life matter to discipleship:

> You shall teach [these laws] diligently to your children, and shall

---

[12] Revelation 22:12.

[13] 1 John 2:6.

[14] *Merriam-Webster*, s.v. "culture," www.merriam-webster.com/dictionary/culture.

talk of them when you sit in your house, and when you walk by the way, and when you lie down, and when you rise. You shall bind them as a sign on your hand, and they shall be as frontlets between your eyes. You shall write them on the doorposts of your house and on your gates.

Our home culture should educate our children in the ways of the Lord, even if children learn math, science, and social studies a few blocks away at the neighborhood school. Likewise, our home culture should educate our children in the ways of the Lord if they are with us all day, learning math, science, and social studies at the kitchen table.

We're tasked with living an authentic gospel-life before our children, teaching and training them with diligence, perseverance, and hope. We're to do this at various times and in various ways, in the morning and in the evening, in every type of situation. Maybe we keep prayer cards in the car and go before the Lord together on the commute to school drop-off. Or we talk with our children after school about the challenges of the day and help them apply Scripture to their situation. In some situations, we can scoot everyone up to the counter and sing a short hymn before breakfast, or we can train our kids to prepare the dinner table for our neighbors in the evening. We can let our love and unity in marriage show them the love and unity between Christ and the church.

Our schooling choice might also be a means to this end, but it probably isn't enough to achieve that end. We must look at our lives, circumstances, personalities, pressures, and passions in light of God's Word and apply its teachings to our situation. We need to evaluate each schooling method's opportunities and limitations, asking how we can best oversee the academic education of our children and disciple them in the gospel of Jesus Christ. We pursue culture-shaping, dependent faithfulness that overflows from an authentic relationship with Jesus Christ. We decide in faith and then keep adjusting when we need to.

I'm not sure how my children will turn out. They might grow up and reject what we're teaching them, or they might grow up and embrace it despite our numerous failures and missteps. But no matter what, my husband's job and mine is to point them to God's narrow path in the best way we know how in the circumstances he has given us. It's to foster a love of God's Word in our everyday lives (regardless of where they go to school), showing them the way of salvation, letting God do his work.

The Tension in Our School Choices

We're left with a tension as Christian parents as we feel the weight of our calling. The weight is that we are asked to teach and train malleable human minds to know the great story of God and salvation through Jesus. We are expected to train and discipline them in obedience and help them see the difference between wisdom and foolishness. This parental job is big and hard and real. No one is going to magically do it for us, and we shouldn't ignore God's commands in passivity or complacency.

The weight of our calling might drive us to extreme worry over the "right" path of school choice unless we acknowledge that we can't fulfill our calling apart from Christ. Every school choice has dangers and errors that we'll have to balance and fill in with right thinking and disciple-making experiences. There are dangers and errors in the hearts of our own children. Ultimately, we can't soften their hearts to the truth. They can fit the mold on the outside while having a heart that is far from God in all we're teaching them. That reality must drive us to rest in his grace.

Jesus is the only person who reconciles the tension between our responsibility and our inability.

Jesus places our identity with himself at the right hand of God, giving us access to a holy Father who loves and accepts us fully. From this perspective, we can view our parental decisions with a deep breath of grateful relief because regardless of what we do next year—whether we set up a homeschool station at our kitchen table, join a co-op with other Christian families, hire a professional teacher to mold our child's mind, enroll in the local private Christian school, find a charter school, or send our child to the public school down the street—we are still with God in Christ.

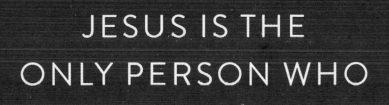

JESUS IS THE
ONLY PERSON WHO
RECONCILES
THE TENSION BETWEEN
OUR RESPONSIBILITY
AND OUR INABILITY

The reality of our acceptance should free space in our hearts and minds to enjoy the path of schooling we choose, knowing it's flawed, as all things are. Then we can disciple and educate our children with wisdom, knowing we will fail, but God is greater. We aren't pressured to "get it right or else" because we trust the one who knows it all and gets it right every time.

We can't sufficiently raise our children according to God's standards with any particular method of schooling. But Christ is sufficient, and he's here to help us disciple our children—whatever schooling method we choose.

DISCUSSION QUESTIONS

1. Imagine the intersections in your child's life. What schooling paths do you see, and what do the destination signs read (if I choose X, then my child will Y)? What gave you those stereotypes, fears, and expectations?

2. What secure hope can you have when you don't know your child's destination in life?

3. Regardless of school choice, how will you infuse the gospel into your child's everyday life, making Christ the culture and aroma of your home?

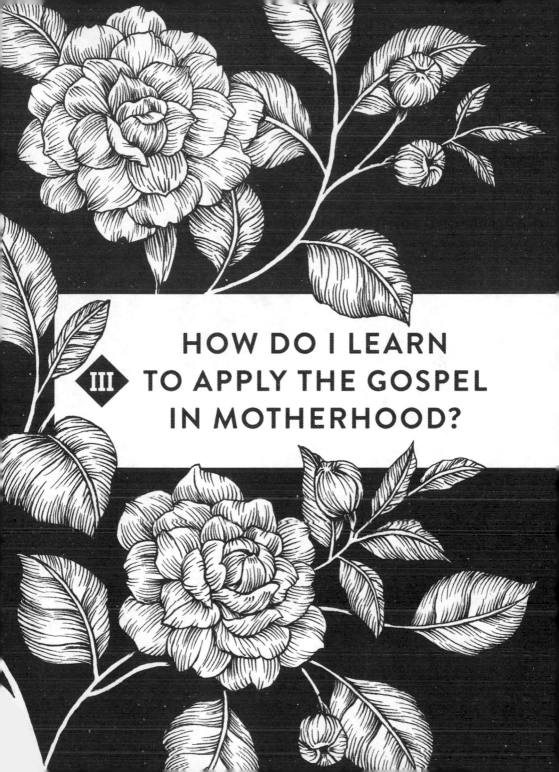

HOW DO I LEARN
III TO APPLY THE GOSPEL
IN MOTHERHOOD?

ARE THE LITTLE YEARS
THE LOST YEARS?

Emily and Laura

Have you ever heard of the 10,000-hour rule?

Some research claims you can become an expert on any topic if you spend 10,000 hours on study and practice. However, the original psychologist behind this research says it's not just doing the same thing over and over (as we often think of practice). It must be what the psychologist calls "deliberate practice."[1] According to his theory, people with little to no talent or base knowledge in a particular area can become top golfers, musicians, free-throw shooters, chess players, and businesspeople.

"Deliberate practice" means developing skills or knowledge in a new area by practicing what you know and stretching yourself just beyond your capabilities. It means getting outside your comfort zone and comfortably living with things you don't yet understand or feel like you can do. It involves being willing to make mistakes and then figuring out how to fix them.

In deliberate practice, you continue learning—not despite the struggle, but because of it.

---

[1] Janie Kliever, "Deliberate Practice: Learn like an Expert," Medium.com, July 14, 2018, https://medium.com/the-crossover-cast/deliberate-practice-learn-like-an-expert-cc3114b8a10e.

If you'd asked us six or seven years ago to write a book like this one, both of us would have laughed. We were new to motherhood and new to everyday gospel application. This skill felt difficult, foreign, and beyond our capacity, and at times, we had thoughts of throwing in the towel. But we knew it was essential to our role as mothers and even more to our calling as believers in Christ. So we persevered, striving to grow in Bible literacy and gospel application amid diaper changes, preschool drop-offs, playdates, and doctors' appointments.

What we know today is a product of applying ourselves in the cracks of time available to us. We admit, in our years of motherhood, there were times we watched Netflix more than we read our Bibles (particularly after each new baby came home). Yet through an overarching time of deep, intentional study and application, or deliberate practice, we pushed ourselves to learn more about God and love him more by studying his Word on our own and in community.

We still have much to learn (and we're definitely not 10,000-hour experts), but we're thankful for how far we've come, even when the growth felt slow. This book is the result of many, many years of on-and-off deliberate practice to know and understand God's Word.

Yet during our short time as moms, we've noticed some people tend to write off the little years. They say things like, "It's okay that you didn't read your Bible or complete your Bible study. You're busy raising children!" We're thankful for their kindness, but these responses imply that margin hours can't add up to much. They don't consider that small efforts can compound toward an eternal purpose.

It's true, we sometimes have valid reasons for not being able to spend time in deep study of God's Word. But we wonder if the most common reason for not engaging in consistent study is not that we don't have time, but that it's…hard?

We don't like the struggle and the sacrifice, so we don't do it.

Let us encourage you—the little years don't have to be the lost years. Those hours (or minutes) add up.

Ordinary Moms, Extraordinary Knowledge, and Love of God

We tend to think that theology, Bible literacy, and gospel application are for pastors and seminary students, or maybe for that super-spiritual woman who disciples us. But the truth is, we're all theologians. We all have ideas about God that inform the way we live our everyday lives.

God wants ordinary people to live gospel-centered lives. As believers, we all have access to the same living and active book, the Bible. We all have the same transforming power of the Holy Spirit, making us like Christ each day. No one receives an extra-special revelation from God. He has designed for every believer to grow in their personal understanding of him through a firsthand knowledge of his Word.

So, what are realistic expectations for growth in God's Word? Perhaps we need to set aside our perfect version of Bible study and engage right where God has us. It's wonderful to enjoy hot coffee with the sunrise in a silent house. We love a quiet time that involves highlighters, cozy blankets, and uninterrupted prayer. But developing a deeper understanding of the gospel is less about crafting the perfect quiet time and more about seeking him throughout our whole day—crumbs, stains, screams, and all. It's firmly, adamantly, stubbornly pursuing God with our whole life. We should try to become 10,000-hour experts on the things of God.

Some might suggest the hours only count if they are uninterrupted, before the kids wake up. But as moms, we don't always have that luxury. Instead of letting that discourage us, let's keep learning where we can, weaving the gospel into our lives until it's so seamless, no one can tell one from the other. It's less like jumping in and out of the pool and more like learning to live in the ocean. It's not getting wet and drying off time and time again, but adapting to a whole new environment, living with full immersion in the things of God. Let God's Word permeate your whole life and soak through all your clothes.

Sometimes it will feel like this progress is arduous. But you grow *because of* the struggle, remember? There will be days when you walk away from your study of God's Word or a conversation with a fellow believer without the answers. You might feel frustration because your beliefs are challenged. You might feel angry or scared because you're cut to the heart and the Holy Spirit is revealing sin in your life. You might want to give up because you think more happiness exists apart from faithful obedience. Transformation doesn't happen overnight, so settle in and get comfortable as God's Spirit grows your understanding and love of the gospel.

Mom, don't underestimate what God is doing in this season. While you are busy washing tiny hands and feet in the bathtub, you can love God and become well-versed in his ways. While you are making snack plates and having picnics in the living room, you can expand your theology. While you are out on a run or playing ring-around-the-rosy, you can deepen in your love of Christ's work on the cross. While you are heading to work, you can apply the gospel to your circumstances. You don't have to wait for an easier season, when your kids are older or even out of the house. You don't have to become a 10,000-hour expert this year, but by God's grace, you can grow and you can change.

A Mom and Her Bible

If you're like us, when it comes to studying the Bible, you're hot and cold. We begin a new Bible study with gusto, only to burn out when we can't find our stash of pretty highlighters. Sometimes our Bible gets stuffed under our van seat for a week. In seasons of consistency in God's Word, we sometimes feel more like we're checking it off our list than developing true devotion to him. Occasionally, we flip open the Bible to a random page in desperation, hoping God will speak to our current situation.

Bible study can be a struggle, especially in the tiring season of young children. But wherever you're at, you can start with consistent reading and thoughtful firsthand study.

Building Bible literacy isn't an easy task.[2] We often come to God's Word hoping it will be like our social media feed, full of inspirational nuggets to carry us

---

[2] Our understanding of Bible literacy has been influenced by many people throughout our lives, including Jen Wilkin. See her book *Women of the Word* (Wheaton, IL: Crossway, 2014).

BY GOD'S GRACE,
YOU CAN GROW
AND YOU CAN
CHANGE

through our day, and feeling disappointed when we don't feel immediately fulfilled or we don't understand what we're reading. We come eager to learn, only
to be interrupted by a toddler waking up from a nap or an older sibling coming to us after a squabble. Our Bible seems too hard, too archaic, too disconnected, too out of touch to speak to our lives, so we give up and turn to other
things for hope.

Yes, Bible study is hard, but it's not without hope. But the answer might not
be what you want to hear.

The key to finding lasting hope and answers to today's questions is through
methodical, intentional study of God's Word. There are many ways to do this.
Entire books have been written on it! We don't have space to go into all the
details, but we've collected our favorite resources on our website at risenmother
hood.com/biblestudytools. In addition, in this chapter we've added a few practical tips for getting started. Growing in Bible literacy is not complicated, but
it's best to have a plan, study with purpose, and keep the long view in mind.

You won't be perfect at it. None of us are. Particularly in these years of raising young children, deliberate practice isn't always realistic. Even though we
need immersion in Scripture more than ever, a move, a new job, a new baby, a
completed adoption, the loss of a loved one, an ailing parent, a sick child, or
something else might cause our time in God's Word to be sporadic. And that's
normal! We've been there.

When this happens, it's important to remember the true meaning of abid-
ing in Christ. For true believers, we always abide with him. Our standing before
God can never change, regardless of whether we read the Bible that day. But at
the same time, if we are truly in Christ, this reality will lead us to abide through
action, with a desire to grow in our understanding of and devotion to God's
Word.[3]

True believers don't rise or fall by the number of hours they've spent reading the Bible that week. Our "bad Bible-reading days" don't need to bring us

---

[3] John 15.

guilt because Jesus bought our freedom with his blood on the cross. But this same sacrifice compels us to make a study plan and keep coming back to God's Word. His love motivates ours, and because the Spirit is at work in us, no season is wasted.

God knows your circumstances. Whether it's listening to the audio Bible in the car, using a reading-plan app during night feedings, or participating in an in-depth study at your church, every deposit can transform you into the likeness of Christ. Every seed can bear fruit. But be stubborn about it. Have some fortitude.

No matter where you're at with Bible reading, no matter how long it's been, we implore you: Pick it back up.

Practical Tips

- Pray before and after you study. Ask God to grow your love for his Word, reveal the true meaning of the text, and transform your life in application.

- Bring your children alongside you and be patient with interruptions. Make disciples while you're growing in your knowledge of God's Word.

- Select one book of the Bible to read over and over again for comprehension, or slowly work your way through the entire Bible to grasp the overarching themes.

Five Years from Now

The 10,000-hours theory has a few other keys to growth to become an expert in anything through deliberate practice. The psychologist behind the research says you need to find a mentor, get feedback, start with the basics, commit for the long haul, and test your skills.[4] This sounds strikingly similar to God's plan

---

[4] K. Anders Ericsson, Michael J. Prietula, and Edward T. Cokely, "The Making of an Expert," *Harvard Business Review*, July 14, 2018, https://hbr.org/2007/07/the-making-of-an-expert.

for growth and discipleship. Living as a gospel expert means committing to a local community of believers, engaging in group Bible study discussions, gaining a foundational knowledge of God's Word, persevering in hard seasons, and applying truth in everyday moments.

If you apply yourself to the study of God's Word through deliberate practice, can you imagine where you'll be in five years? Take our word for it from personal experience—you'll be a different person, even if you have the same circumstances.

With that in mind, let's enjoy our ideal quiet time when we can but also keep our Bibles open at the breakfast table, on the bathroom vanity, and on the coffee table. Let's fill our bookshelves with gospel-rich literature made for adults and children. Let's meet with godly friends who are also pursuing God so we can discuss how the gospel applies to our personal lives and the culture around us. Let's sing silly songs and serious songs that help us remember deep truths about good doctrine.

Let's turn on an audio Bible app in the car on the way to school or pull our kids up to the couch while we finish reading—giving them some fun toys to play with nearby. Let's get involved in a local church where we'll find women to pour into us and women to pour into. When we're folding laundry or commuting home from work, let's listen to theologically sound podcasts, sermons, and conference talks. In all of it, let's think critically and deliberately about what we hear, comparing it to the truth of God's Word.

Let's start learning again when we stop. Let's get back up when we fall off. Let's bask in God's grace and ask him for grit to keep going. Give it five years. We would guess you'll be pleasantly surprised by the fruit—all sown in the years we're told are lost.

Mold Your Heart and Mind to God

Growing in Bible literacy in the little years is a bit like raising kids. You invest day after day, sometimes feeling like nothing is happening. But over time, you see them change. By God's grace, they *can* voice their grateful heart by saying

THE
LITTLE YEARS
ARE NOT THE
LOST YEARS

please and thank you, they *can* feel conviction for hitting their sister and apologize, and they *can* have a heart for those who are left out and invite them to play.

It's the same for you. You might feel like the input isn't initially yielding change, but over time you'll find you can recall applicable Bible passages. That familiarity allows you to rehearse the gospel story to yourself. Then one day, when you're feeling anxious, you automatically start putting life and truth together.

You can start to see the Bible as one big story explained in a lot of different ways over a long period of time. You can recognize when something you hear from a friend doesn't align with the truth of God's Word. You can start spotting half-truths in pretty squares on your Instagram feed or the latest Christian bestsellers. You can even understand hard parts of the Old Testament!

In time, by God's grace, all this learning, communing, and meditating makes a difference. It's not about earning knowledge, but about storing up God's Word in our hearts so our hearts begin to mold into his. We will come to love what he loves, care for what he cares for, and live out what he has called us to.

No matter what, remember that growing in Bible literacy and knowledge of the gospel is not just for the smartest of the smart. The gospel is for everyone—for every mom. For moms who stay home, work from home, or work outside the home (and everything in between). The gospel is for poor moms, rich moms, and middle-class moms. The gospel is for moms of every skin tone and ethnic background. The gospel is for the weary mom, the perfectionist mom, and the doubting mom. The gospel is for the mom who feels like she's doing a good enough job and for the mom who feels like the worst mom on the planet.

Change might be slow, but it's not a contest. Let us reiterate—the gospel is for you, and God's power can work in anyone in any season of life. The little years are not the lost years.

So now that you have the building blocks for growing in your knowledge and love of God, let's talk about how you can apply that truth in everyday life. How you can remember the gospel on your best days and on the days when you've completely blown it. It's commonly referred to as preaching the gospel to yourself.

Or you can just think of it as living Risen Motherhood.

DISCUSSION QUESTIONS

1. What excuses do you make about faithfulness in the little years? How might your expectations of growth in God's Word need to change in this season?

2. How does the gospel offer you freedom from guilt yet motivate you to be stubborn—and keep coming back to God's Word?

3. Are there areas of Bible literacy and gospel growth that you choose not to pursue because they're hard? What adjustments might you make to invest in Bible literacy in the amounts of time you have available?

LIVING RISEN MOTHERHOOD

Emily and Laura

W e've seen each other through some ugly moments in motherhood. We've battled pride and embarrassment at snack time, when one person's child ate the carrots while the other person's child turned up their nose. We've watched each other snap at the child in the other room instead of getting up to parent in kindness. We've witnessed each other's children melt down for good and bad reasons because of our lack of training and despite our efforts. We've compared bedtime routines at family gatherings when some children went straight to sleep while the others tested limits.

We've also seen each other through painful moments in motherhood. Seasons of pursuing adoption and seasons of ending the process without bringing any new children into the family. We've talked each other through fears during NICU stays, developmental evaluations, allergy testing, and vision screenings. When fears became broken realities, we've prayed for each other. When surgeries came, wheelchairs arrived, and complex medical treatments dragged on, we've even laughed together because it hurt too much to do anything else.

By God's grace, we've seen hopeful triumphs in motherhood. Children who once reacted with outbursts of rage now looking out for the interests of the weak and small. We've celebrated little ones who believe the gospel with faith. We've watched God work through years of pleading, producing breakthrough and change in areas of habitual sin and struggle.

Through the sins, struggles, and joys, we've preached the gospel to each other, and we've learned to preach it to ourselves.[1]

No, we've never taken each other to a church building, taking turns at the pulpit. We preach to ourselves in conversations over hot cups of coffee, video calls after bedtime, and text messages in the afternoon. In living rooms, at restaurants, on vacation, on family holidays, and on walks around the park—we've reminded each other of the truth of the gospel.

We've affirmed God's good design to each other. "Yes, God is gracious to give us healthy bodies." "Yes, I see the Holy Spirit working in your child's heart." "Yes, God is generous and kind to meet all our needs."

We've affirmed the hardship of life under the sun. "No, it shouldn't be this painful." "No, you shouldn't have treated your child that way." "No, your circumstances aren't easy."

We've remembered the freedom available through the sacrifice of Christ on our behalf that compels us to obey God in hard things. "I know you snapped at your kids, but you can repent. His mercies are new. Trust he is working to grow you to be more like him."

We've hoped together in Christ's resurrection and what it means for our future. "This is all going to be made right." "This will end, and someday he'll wipe away every tear."

Preaching the gospel to one another and to ourselves is an exercise in ongoing redemptive conversation. It's Spirit-led sentences strung together, weaving the beauty of the gospel into the fabric of our relationship.

Maybe you're thinking, "I don't know how to make connections in that way"

---

[1] The word "preach" has many connotations. Most of us think of preachers standing behind church pulpits. However, in the New Testament, the word is often used more broadly, referring to someone who proclaims the gospel in a public way. Sometimes this is done with the authority of apostleship or modernly, in the context of being an elder or a pastor. Other times, it's just a general minister of the gospel (ordinary men and women sharing Jesus). In this book, we're using the word "preach" to simply mean proclaiming the gospel to ourselves and to our peers, reminding each other of truth and pointing ourselves and each other back to the gospel.

or "I don't have a vocabulary like that." Maybe you can't think of a friend who would talk with you about these things. Or maybe you recall a time when you tried to speak gospel truth but someone rolled their eyes.

Don't lose heart! We know it's not easy, and at times it feels unnatural. But we want to encourage you to try and leave you with a few practical tips and examples for preaching the gospel to yourself and to those around you. We are not perfect at it. Sometimes we see our sin, but instead of repenting right away, we let days and weeks go by. Sometimes we're so eager to help one another that we give each other commiserating advice instead of pointing each other to Christ. But we'll still try to share what's helping us. We want to be doers of the Word, not just hearers, so we invite you to take what you're learning and put it into practice wherever you are.

Preaching the gospel to yourself means helping your head inform your heart, reorienting it around the things of Christ. Preaching the gospel to yourself is living Risen Motherhood.

Remember the Gospel

Each year, our children attend Cousin Camp at Grandma and Papa Jensen's house. It's a multi-night extravaganza (although mysteriously, it's gotten shorter every year). This annual event includes sleeping bags, late-night runs for ice cream, field trips, water play, decorations, games, Bible lessons, and custom T-shirts. Our kids especially love the T-shirts because they're a perpetual badge of honor—proof they attended Cousin Camp and they're in the family. If any of our kids sees a cousin in their Cousin Camp shirt, they start talking about their best memories and asking about next year's camp.

"Where's my shirt, Mommy? I want to wear mine too!"

"Remember the day we went to the pool? I want to go back!"

"Aunt Barb was there. Is she coming back this year?"

Sometimes their questions and excitement rise to a level that is nearly out of control, but we're not surprised by the commotion. Cousin Camp is a memorable thing they share with their family. It's fun from the past and something to look forward to in the future. Why wouldn't they talk about it any chance they got?

Although none of us are likely to start walking around with "Gospel Camp" T-shirts on, we hope that if we did wear them, they would incite the same response.

"Oh, you know Jesus too! What was your story? How did you come to trust him? What was it like when you repented and believed?"

"How can I pray for you? Where do you need encouragement?"

"Aren't you so excited to see Jesus face-to-face someday? What do you think it will be like?"

Okay, very cheesy, but you get the gist. When we've experienced the most exciting relationship with the best parent in the best family we'll ever know, wouldn't it make sense to reminisce?

Thinking about the gospel, talking about the gospel, and preaching the gospel starts with remembering. Remembering how perfect and holy God is. Remembering our sin and what we deserved. Remembering how God pursued us and saved us when we were still sinners. Remembering how he gave us new eyes and new hearts that love to serve him. Remembering Jesus' example of loving God and others. Remembering that he's coming back for us.

These memories overflow into words and actions. Once we've meditated on the amazing nature of the gospel and are held captive by the grace of God, there should be no choice but to share it. Then we can rehearse and apply those truths to our lives more and more.

Practical Tips

- Listen to an audio version of Scripture while you're getting ready for the day, making your commute, or cleaning the house. Pause and think about who God is and what he's done and is doing.

- Ask a friend, "Can you tell me how you came to put your faith in

Christ? I don't think I've ever heard that story." (Sometimes it only takes one conversation to get the ball rolling!)

Rehearse the Gospel

Before we go on a family outing, it's common to see us rehearse expectations with our children with the thumbs-up / thumbs-down game.

"Okay, kids. We're almost to the park. Can you stay on the path?" (Thumbs up.)

"Should you run in the parking lot?" (Thumbs down.)

"What about having fun? Can you have fun?" (Thumbs up…and lots of squealing.)

The purpose of the thumbs-up / thumbs-down game isn't to train the children in something completely new. They've been to the park often enough to know the rules. We want to play out real scenarios, rehearsing how our kids should respond so it's fresh in their minds. Our hope is that when the car comes to a halt and they all jump out, they're prepared and remember how to obey in that specific situation.

None of us do an adult form of the thumbs-up / thumbs-down game that asks, "Should you yell at your kids when you get frustrated? Should you nag your husband about that chore he hasn't completed? Is it okay to hug your kids today?" (We hope you know the answers to those things.) But it's still helpful to rehearse the truths we know so we're ready to obey in our everyday situations.

This is best done in relationship with others, but we can also rehearse the gospel on our own. When we rehearse with others, we discuss truth from God's Word and prepare one another by discussing specific scenarios. This also includes talking about the gospel itself, affirming ways we see God's image in one another, and acknowledging sin and brokenness. We discuss the things we're thankful for and apply hope to hard places. We talk openly about God's future promises and how those apply.

Practical Tips

- Get involved in your local church by joining a Bible study, a small group, a mom's meet-up, or something similar. Don't just show up, but engage in conversation and be persistent about forming relationships with people who love Jesus and want to grow in the gospel.

- Read or listen to a gospel-centered resource with one or two friends so you can all practice deepening your conversation to the heart level. Be bold—it's okay to be the first one to suggest something like this.

Apply the Gospel

We all share a lot of the same expectations for our kids, but the application is different for each child in different situations. Kids have to get used to gray areas.

"Should you run? In some situations, no. If you are in a crowd at the state fair, don't run. But if you're playing tag, do run. If you are in a parking lot, don't run. But if you are at the playground, it's okay to run." So if a child is asking, "Is it okay to run?" the reality is…it depends. And some kids may have different answers in the same situation. "It might be okay for your cousin to run, but you need to stay beside Mommy because I asked you to carry a bag from the car." In some situations running is great, but in others it's dangerous.

We sometimes ask our own children to do different things. The toddler must hold our hand or be carried while the older children walk ahead. Depending on age, awareness of danger, ability to stay close to Mom and Dad, and so on, a child might have to do any range of things, from riding strapped into a stroller to skipping with a pack of cousins. It's hard to explain to a child why sometimes they are in the stroller and other times they aren't. But either way, as parents, we have a good plan for their safety. We try to help them discern what we're asking in each situation and why we're asking it.

GOD WANTS
US TO DO WHAT
IMAGES HIM
MOST CLEARLY,
WORSHIPS HIM
MOST FULLY,
AND LOVES
OTHER IMAGE-
BEARERS MOST
SACRIFICIALLY

When it comes to gospel application, it feels sticky. "I've remembered the gospel—I've thought about what God did for me in Christ. I've rehearsed the gospel—I've talked to myself and to others about how this works itself out in different situations. But what about application? How do I know how these truths change me in this very moment?"

Much like it is with our children, it comes down to obedience, principles, and heart attitudes. We seek to obey biblical commands and principles as we understand our hearts and God's overarching intentions. Many things boil down to the greatest commandments—to love God with all our heart, soul, mind, and strength, and to love our neighbor as ourselves. God wants us to do what images him most clearly, worships him most fully, and loves other image-bearers most sacrificially. He also wants us to have hearts that desire to obey him and seek understanding to that end—hearts that put his interests for our lives before our own.

We sometimes wish this could be like uncovering a rare treasure or going on a Bible scavenger hunt until we discover a hidden message about whether to try to have another baby, take a new job, or move to a new town. But actually it's not that complicated:

"Give thanks in all circumstances; for this is the will of God in Christ Jesus for you" (1 Thessalonians 5:18).

"Look carefully then how you walk, not as unwise but as wise, making the best use of the time, because the days are evil. Therefore do not be foolish, but understand what the will of the Lord is. And do not get drunk with wine, for that is debauchery, but be filled with the Spirit, addressing one another in psalms and hymns and spiritual songs, singing and making melody to the Lord with your heart, giving thanks always and for everything to God the Father in the name of our Lord Jesus Christ" (Ephesians 5:15-20).

Give thanks. Prayerfully understand what it means to make the best use of the time he's given you on Earth. Don't numb the pain of the fall with improper use of God's gifts, but engage in Christian community, helping others remember the gospel, rehearse the gospel, and give thanks for it as we all live in Christ. Pray and ask God to help you apply the gospel, and follow through by acting on what you know. Trust God to teach and correct you through his Word, his church, and his Spirit.

Practical Tips

- Journal what God is teaching you through his Word and prayerfully write out ways those truths might impact your life each day.
- Engage a mentor and ask her questions about gospel application.

Gospel Life Is Community Life

Here's the thing about books, podcasts, Bible teachers, and Bible study groups you find online: They can be immensely helpful when it comes to learning, but they are incapable of seeing your personal life and speaking the gospel into your everyday situations.

In this book, we've done our best to imagine what you might be facing. We've tried to talk about principles that have general application to the greatest amount of people. But often, you need more help with your unique situation. When you're in the same conflict with your husband again, when you've tried all the discipline strategies and nothing works, or when you're not sure what to do for schooling next fall, you're likely to need another believer's help. Someone who sees your life and knows the context of your testimony, your relationships, and your struggles. Someone who can help you work them out with prayer and wisdom.

As you work out application with others, remember that people have major flaws. Gospel communities aren't insulated from sin and hurt. No one's counsel should contradict the Bible, but a good group of gospel-centered believers—people who are striving for the glory of God in all things—is essential to gospel application in everyday life.

Final Hope

No matter what kind of day, week, month, or year you've had, it doesn't have to determine your future. If you know your inability to save yourself, have confessed your sin, and placed your hope in Jesus, you have a new identity. You've been adopted.[2] Not by any works of your own but by grace through faith.[3] You've been given a new name and an imperishable inheritance kept in heaven for you.[4] Someday, Jesus will return, and you'll be physically and spiritually restored to new life forever. We'll see the pains of today—the hard doctor's appointments, the stress over food allergies, the massive pre-nap tantrums, the arguments over food, the unwanted diagnosis—in the perspective of our eternally good Father and his eternally good plan for his people.

If you've learned anything from this book, we hope it's a clear presentation of the good news of Jesus Christ, which is the power of salvation for those who hear and respond. We pray that if you haven't responded to that before, you'll respond now. Don't wait until you've cleaned up your act, until you've started reading the Bible and praying more, or until you are a "better" mom. Come as you are—humble, lowly, and in need of a Savior who needs nothing from you. He loved you before you ever loved him.

No matter where your relationship is with God, remember that when you repent and believe in Jesus, the Holy Spirit grafts you into the living vine, Jesus himself. As you abide in him, you will begin to change and produce fruit that comes from an authentic attachment to that life-giving vine. As the fruit of the Spirit grows in your life, you will start to love others like Christ has loved you. You'll have the joy of the Lord in hard circumstances. Your soul will know true peace when everything else feels chaotic. You'll show patience with incessant children and respond to unfair treatment and annoyance with kindness. You'll

---

[2] Romans 8:15.

[3] Ephesians 2:8.

[4] 1 Peter 1:4.

do good to others even when they don't do good to you. You'll be faithful in the unseen things, treat small hearts with gentleness, and be self-controlled.

Is motherhood like that even possible? Not perfectly, of course, but progressively. As you remain in him, you will change. And it's not too late to start or begin again. Right now.

We pray that you relentlessly put your hope in Christ over and over again, receiving hope in the everyday moments today and forevermore.

DISCUSSION QUESTIONS

1. What messages do you currently preach to yourself in the hard moments of motherhood? Where did these messages come from, and how do they compare with the gospel?

2. What tools and strategies will you use to remind yourself of gospel truth next time you're facing stress, fear, or guilt as a mom?

3. How has considering gospel application in the everyday moments of motherhood changed the way you see God, yourself, your family, and your community? Where will you apply this hope next?

ABOUT THE AUTHORS

Emily Jensen and **Laura Wifler** are the cofounders of the Risen Motherhood ministry and cohosts of the chart-topping podcast. They are also in the trenches of motherhood, right alongside their readers. With a combination of accessibility, relatability, and solid biblical knowledge, Emily and Laura have a knack for simplifying complex scriptural truths, relating and applying them to everyday life. God has consistently and powerfully used the voices of these two moms to captivate women around the world with the gospel. As sisters-in-law, Emily and Laura both live in central Iowa with their families.

Connect with Us:

🔘 emily___jensen

🔘 laurawifler

THE RISEN MOTHERHOOD COMMUNITY

In a world full of opinions, how-tos, and silver-bullet solutions, Risen Motherhood offers a countercultural message to relieve the world's burdens placed on moms through the good news of the gospel. At Risen Motherhood, we believe moms can faithfully live out their calling in freedom as they know God's will through his Word. To this end, Risen Motherhood creates podcasts, articles, and free Bible study resources to equip, encourage, and challenge mothers to live in the light of the gospel.

Join the Risen Motherhood Community:

RisenMotherhood.com

 risenmotherhood

Risen Motherhood

RisenMotherhood.com/book